The Haggadah

transliterated & translated
with instructions
& commentary

© 2002 The Judaica Press, Inc.
First printing 2002
Second printing 2003
Third printing 2006

ISBN-13: 978-1-880582-60-2
ISBN-10: 1-880582-60-0

The publisher is grateful to Shimon Apisdorf, author of the *Survival Kit* series,
for permission to use his works in the preparation of the commentary for this Haggadah.

Transliteration: Yaakov Smith
Typography and Design: B. Goldman and Z. Berkowitz
Cover Illustration: Ilene Winn-Lederer

THE JUDAICA PRESS, INC.
JUDAICAPRESS.COM

123 Ditmas Avenue
Brooklyn, New York 11218
718-972-6200 / 800-972-6201
info@judaicapress.com

Manufactured in the United States of America

Transliteration Key

Letter combination	Should be read as in:
ay	p**lay**
ai	**ai**sle
i	l**i**ft
ee	f**ee**t
oo	b**oo**t
e	sh**e**d
a	qu**a**lity
ch	Ba**ch**
o	m**o**st
u	p**u**t
' (apostrophe)	the soft **a** in surf**a**ce

✿ בדיקת חמץ ✿

Bedikat Chametz
Search for the Leaven

On the evening before the Passover seder, the final preparation is done by searching for leaven (known in Hebrew as *chametz*) throughout the house. (If Passover begins on Saturday evening, the search is conducted the previous Thursday evening.) This search, called *bedikat chametz*, is done by candlelight. In places where there may be flammable material or in close quarters (i.e., closets or under beds), a flashlight is permissible and advisable. Customarily, ten small pieces of bread are placed around the house before the search so that leaven will be found during the search. A feather and a wooden spoon are often used to gather the new-found leaven into a bag.

Before beginning the search, we recite the following blessing:

בָּרוּךְ אַתָּה יְיָ אֱלֹהֵינוּ מֶלֶךְ הָעוֹלָם, אֲשֶׁר קִדְּשָׁנוּ בְּמִצְוֹתָיו, וְצִוָּנוּ עַל בִּעוּר חָמֵץ.

Baruch atah Ado-nai, Elo-haynoo, melech ha-olam, asher kid'sha-noo b'mitzvotav, v'tzee-vanoo al bee-oor chamaytz.

Blessed are you, Lord our God, King of the universe, Who has sanctified us with His commandments, and commanded us concerning the removal of leaven.

Every room of the house is searched. After the search has been conducted and the remaining leaven has been wrapped up, the following statement is recited:

כָּל חֲמִירָא וַחֲמִיעָה דְּאִכָּא בִרְשׁוּתִי דְּלָא חֲמִתֵּהּ וּדְלָא בְעַרְתֵּהּ וּדְלָא יְדַעְנָא לֵיהּ לִבָּטֵל וְלֶהֱוֵי הֶפְקֵר כְּעַפְרָא דְאַרְעָא.

Kol cha-mee-ra vachamee-ah d'eeka veershootee, d'la cha-meetay oo-d'la vee-artay, oo-d'la y'dana lay leebatayl v'leh-hevay hefkayr, k'afra d'ara.

Any type of leaven that may still be in my possession, that I have not seen or not removed, or that I do not know about, let it be considered nullified and ownerless, like the dust of the earth.

On the morning following *bedikat chametz* (if Passover begins on Saturday evening, then this is done on Friday morning), all of the remaining leaven in the

house is burned, including the leaven found on the search of the previous night.

The following statement is then recited:

כָּל חֲמִירָא וַחֲמִיעָה דְּאִכָּא בִּרְשׁוּתִי דַּחֲזִיתֵהּ וּדְלָא חֲזִיתֵהּ, דַּחֲמִתֵּהּ וּדְלָא חֲמִתֵּהּ, דְּבִעַרְתֵּהּ וּדְלָא בִעַרְתֵּהּ, לִבָּטֵל וְלֶהֱוֵי הֶפְקֵר כְּעַפְרָא דְאַרְעָא.

Kol cha-mee-ra vachamee-ah d'eeka veershootee, dacha-zeetay oo-d'la cha-zeetay, dacha-meetay oo-d'la cha-meetay, d'vee-artay oo-d'la vee-artay, leebatayl v'le-hevay hefkayr, k'afra d'ara.

Any type of leaven that may still be in my possession, that I may or may not have seen, found or removed, let it be considered nullified and ownerless, like the dust of the earth.

ערוב תבשלין
Eruv Tavshilin
Mixing of Cooked Foods

When the first day of Passover falls on a Thursday, in order to be able to cook on Friday for Shabbat, we prepare something called *Eruv Tavshilin* on the Wednesday afternoon before the festival begins. (Torah law ordinarily permits cooking on a Yom Tov day for that day alone, not in advance for the next festival day.)

Take a piece of matzah and any cooked food—such as a piece of meat or fish, or a cooked egg—place them on a plate, raise it, and recite the following blessing and statement:

בָּרוּךְ אַתָּה יְיָ אֱלֹהֵינוּ מֶלֶךְ הָעוֹלָם, אֲשֶׁר קִדְּשָׁנוּ בְּמִצְוֹתָיו, וְצִוָּנוּ עַל מִצְוַת עֵרוּב.

Baruch atah Ado-nai, Elo-haynoo, melech ha-olam, asher kid'sha-noo b'mitzvotav, v'tzee-vanoo al mitzvat ay-roov.

Blessed are you, Lord our God, King of the universe, Who has sanctified us with His commandments, and commanded us concerning the commandment of the eruv.

בְּהֲדֵין עֵרוּבָא יְהֵא שָׁרֵא לָנָא לַאֲפוּיֵי וּלְבַשּׁוּלֵי וּלְאַטְמוּנֵי וּלְאַדְלוּקֵי
שְׁרָגָא וּלְתַקָּנָא וּלְמֶעְבַּד כָּל צָרְכָנָא, מִיּוֹמָא טָבָא לְשַׁבַּתָּא [לָנוּ
וּלְכָל יִשְׂרָאֵל הַדָּרִים בָּעִיר הַזֹּאת].

Ba-hadayn ay'roova, y'hay sha-ray lanah la-afoo-yay, oo-l'vashoo-lay, oo-l'atmoonay, oo-l'ad-lookay sh'ra-ga, oo-l'takana oo-l'meh-bahd kol tzar-chana, mee-yoma tava l'sha-bata (lanoo, oo-l'chol yisra'ayl hada-rim ba-eer ha-zot).

With this eruv, let it be permitted for us to bake, cook, and keep food warm, to light candles, to tend to and take care of all our needs, from the festival to the Shabbat (for us, and for all Jews that dwell in this city).

⤠ הדלקת נרות ⤟

Hadlakat Neirot
Lighting the Candles

Like Shabbat candles, the purpose of candles for the Yom Tov is to bring light and joy into the house. The standard time for candle lighting is customarily eighteen minutes before sunset. Generally the candles are lit near the table where you will have the seder so you can enjoy their glow during the meal.

The candles are lit and the following two blessings are recited.
When Passover falls on Shabbat, the words in brackets are added.

בָּרוּךְ אַתָּה יְיָ אֱלֹהֵינוּ מֶלֶךְ הָעוֹלָם, אֲשֶׁר קִדְּשָׁנוּ בְּמִצְוֹתָיו, וְצִוָּנוּ
לְהַדְלִיק נֵר שֶׁל [שַׁבָּת וְשֶׁל] יוֹם טוֹב.

Baruch atah Ado-nai, Elo-haynoo, melech ha-olam, asher kid'sha-noo b'mitzvotav, v'tzee-vanoo l'hadleek nayr shel [Shabbat v'shel] Yom Tov.

Blessed are you Lord, our God, King of the universe, Who has sanctified us with His commandments, and has commanded us to kindle the light of [Shabbat and of] the Festival.

בָּרוּךְ אַתָּה יְיָ, אֱלֹהֵינוּ מֶלֶךְ הָעוֹלָם, שֶׁהֶחֱיָנוּ וְקִיְּמָנוּ וְהִגִּיעָנוּ לַזְּמַן הַזֶּה:

Baruch atah, Ado-nai, Elo-haynoo, melech ha-olam, she-heche-yanoo, v'kee-y'manoo, v'heegee-anoo la-z'man ha-zeh.

Blessed are you, Lord, our God, King of the universe, Who has kept us alive, preserved us, and enabled us to reach this season.

✑ Arranging the Seder Plate ✑

Before the seder begins, the following items are arranged on a plate. You can buy a special seder plate at Jewish book shops or just use any large plate.

1. **Zeroa**—a roasted shankbone;
2. **Beitzah**—a hard-boiled egg;
3. **Marror**—bitter herbs (commonly either horseradish or romaine lettuce);
4. **Charoset**—a mixture of wine, chopped nuts, apples, and cinnamon;
5. **Karpas**—a green vegetable (such as celery, parsley, or potatoes).

Passover, the original multimedia experience, presents us with a dazzling array of objects and images, each of which directs our thoughts and feelings towards another nuance of the potential contained within the entire seder experience. Each of the seder plate items is a touchstone that steers our attention towards a deeper understanding of Passover, of being Jewish, and of ourselves.

What else you need:
1. Three matzot (plural for matzah), covered individually. (Special matzah covers with three compartments are available at Jewish book stores.)
2. A cup of wine in front of each participant, plus a supply of additional wine to refill the cups three more times.
3. A container of salt-water.
4. A cup for Elijah—a large goblet in the center of the table.
5. A pillow or cushion for each participant, so that everyone can recline during certain parts of the seder.

❧ The Order of the Seder ❧

*The Hebrew word for order is "seder." For over three thousand years, this evening
has followed a very particular order. The following are the details of what's planned
for the evening. Each word and ritual is laden with meaning and many people have the
custom to recite these words before performing each of the appropriate rituals.*

Kadesh	קַדֵּשׁ	Recite the Kiddush
Urechatz	וּרְחַץ	Wash hands
Karpas	כַּרְפַּס	Eat a vegetable dipped in salt water
Yachatz	יַחַץ	Break the middle matzah
Maggid	מַגִּיד	Recite the Haggadah
Rachtzah	רָחְצָה	Wash hands before eating matzah
Motzi	מוֹצִיא	Recite the blessing "Hamotzi"
Matzah	מַצָּה	Recite the blessing "Al achilat matzah" & eat the matzah
Marror	מָרוֹר	Eat the bitter herbs dipped in charoset
Korech	כּוֹרֵךְ	Eat the matzah and marror sandwich
Shulchan Orech	שֻׁלְחָן עוֹרֵךְ	Eat the holiday meal
Tzafun	צָפוּן	Eat the Afikomen
Barech	בָּרֵךְ	Recite Grace after Meals
Hallel	הַלֵּל	Recite psalms of praise
Nirtzah	נִרְצָה	Our seder service is accepted and concluded

⸙ קַדֵּשׁ ⸙
Kadesh
Recite the Kiddush

After all the preparations, quiet falls on the house on the evening of the seder. Traditionally, one goes to synagogue services or waits until the sky is dark enough that at least three stars can be viewed. The Kiddush is then recited. Once the Kiddush is recited, the seder has officially begun.

The majesty of the evening is hinted at when each seder participant's cup is poured by someone else. This tradition symbolizes our transformation from slaves to a free people. In addition, our seder table is considered full when we have invited strangers to join us—in fact, as we will see later, inviting guests is an integral part of the seder.

Each man and woman and young adult attending the seder is fully partakes in this ritual and so each person must have a full glass of wine placed on the table in front of them.

Each person at the seder recites the blessing on the wine.
On Friday night, begin here. On other nights, begin on page 11.

וַיְהִי עֶרֶב וַיְהִי בֹקֶר

יוֹם הַשִּׁשִּׁי, וַיְכֻלּוּ הַשָּׁמַיִם וְהָאָרֶץ וְכָל צְבָאָם: וַיְכַל אֱלֹהִים בַּיּוֹם הַשְּׁבִיעִי, מְלַאכְתּוֹ אֲשֶׁר עָשָׂה, וַיִּשְׁבֹּת בַּיּוֹם הַשְּׁבִיעִי, מִכָּל מְלַאכְתּוֹ אֲשֶׁר עָשָׂה: וַיְבָרֶךְ אֱלֹהִים אֶת יוֹם הַשְּׁבִיעִי, וַיְקַדֵּשׁ אֹתוֹ, כִּי בוֹ שָׁבַת מִכָּל מְלַאכְתּוֹ, אֲשֶׁר בָּרָא אֱלֹהִים לַעֲשׂוֹת:

On the night of Passover, Jews all over the world enter a magical place, a place filled with special foods, with family and friends and exciting stories. And Kadesh is the entrance to that magical place.

Va-y'hee erev va-y'hee vo-ker Yom ha-sheeshee. Va-y'chooloo ha-shama-yim v'ha-aretz v'chol tz'va-am. Va-y'chal Elo-him ba-yom ha-sh'vee-ee m'lachto asher asah, va-yishbot ba-yom ha-sh'vee-ee meekol m'lachto asher asah. Va-y'va-rech Elo-him et yom ha-sh'vee-ee va-y'ka-daysh oto, kee vo shavat meekol m'lachto, asher bara Elo-him la-assot.

It was evening and it was morning on the sixth day. And the heavens and the earth were completed and all their hosts. And God completed on the seventh day all the work that He had done, and He abstained on the seventh day from all the work that He had done. And God blessed the seventh day and sanctified it, for thereon He abstained from all His work that God had created to do.

On all nights other than Friday night begin here; on Friday night include the words in parentheses.

סַבְרִי מָרָנָן וְרַבָּנָן וְרַבּוֹתַי:

בָּרוּךְ אַתָּה יְיָ, אֱלֹהֵינוּ מֶלֶךְ הָעוֹלָם, בּוֹרֵא פְּרִי הַגָּפֶן:

בָּרוּךְ אַתָּה יְיָ, אֱלֹהֵינוּ מֶלֶךְ הָעוֹלָם, אֲשֶׁר בָּחַר בָּנוּ מִכָּל עָם, וְרוֹמְמָנוּ מִכָּל לָשׁוֹן, וְקִדְּשָׁנוּ בְּמִצְוֹתָיו, וַתִּתֶּן לָנוּ יְיָ אֱלֹהֵינוּ בְּאַהֲבָה (שַׁבָּתוֹת לִמְנוּחָה וּ)מוֹעֲדִים לְשִׂמְחָה, חַגִּים וּזְמַנִּים לְשָׂשׂוֹן אֶת יוֹם (הַשַּׁבָּת הַזֶּה וְאֶת יוֹם) חַג הַמַּצּוֹת הַזֶּה. זְמַן חֵרוּתֵנוּ, (בְּאַהֲבָה) מִקְרָא קֹדֶשׁ, זֵכֶר לִיצִיאַת מִצְרָיִם. כִּי בָנוּ בָחַרְתָּ וְאוֹתָנוּ קִדַּשְׁתָּ מִכָּל הָעַמִּים. (וְשַׁבָּת) וּמוֹעֲדֵי קָדְשֶׁךָ (בְּאַהֲבָה וּבְרָצוֹן) בְּשִׂמְחָה וּבְשָׂשׂוֹן הִנְחַלְתָּנוּ: בָּרוּךְ אַתָּה יְיָ, מְקַדֵּשׁ (הַשַּׁבָּת וְ)יִשְׂרָאֵל וְהַזְּמַנִּים:

Savree mara-nan v'raba-nan v'ra-botai:

Baruch atah Ado-nai, Elo-haynoo, melech ha-olam, boray p'ree haga-fen.

Baruch atah Ado-nai, Elo-haynoo, melech ha-olam, asher bachar ba-noo meekol am, v'ro-m'-manoo meekol lashon, v'kid'sha-noo b'mitzvotav. Va-tee-ten la-noo, Ado-nai, Elo-haynoo, b'a-havah (shabbatot li-m'noocha, oo-) mo-adim l'simchah, chagim oo-z'manim l'sason (et yom ha-shabbat ha-zeh v') et yom chag ha-matzot hazeh, z'man chay-roo-taynoo, (b'a-havah) mikra ko-desh, zaycher leetzee-at mitzra-yim. Kee va-noo vacharta, v'ota-noo keedashta meekol ha-amim, (v'shab-bat) oo-mo-aday kodshecha (b'a-havah oo-v'ratzon) b'simcha oo-v'sason hinchalta-noo. Baruch atah, Adonai, m'ka-daysh (ha-shab-bat, v') yisra-ayl, v'ha-z'manim.

Attention our masters and our teachers:

Blessed are You, Lord, our God, King of the universe, Who created the fruit of the vine.

Blessed are You, Lord, our God, King of the universe, Who has chosen us from every nation, exalted us above every language, and sanctified us with His commandments. You have given us, Lord, our God, with love (Shabbatot for rest, and) festivals for happiness, holidays and seasons for joy, this day of (Shabbat and this day of) the holiday of matzot, the season of our freedom (with love) a holy assembly, commemorating the Exodus from Egypt. For You have chosen us, and You have sanctified us above all the nations, and Your (Shabbat and) holy festivals (with love and favor) in happiness and joy You granted us. Blessed are you, Lord, Who sanctifies (Shabbat,) Israel, and the seasons.

Traditionally, we recline to the left when drinking the four cups of wine at the seder. Even a pauper is obligated to do so. Although many people tend to mistakenly equate freedom only with wealth, the fact that we all recline on seder night makes the statement: It's not how much you have that makes you free, but what you do with what you have.

On Saturday evening add the following two blessings.
We look towards the Yom Tov candles as we recite this blessing.
(On all other nights, we skip to the blessing below.)

בָּרוּךְ אַתָּה יְיָ, אֱלֹהֵינוּ מֶלֶךְ הָעוֹלָם, בּוֹרֵא מְאוֹרֵי הָאֵשׁ:

בָּרוּךְ אַתָּה יְיָ, אֱלֹהֵינוּ מֶלֶךְ הָעוֹלָם, הַמַּבְדִּיל בֵּין קֹדֶשׁ לְחֹל, בֵּין אוֹר לְחֹשֶׁךְ, בֵּין יִשְׂרָאֵל לָעַמִּים, בֵּין יוֹם הַשְּׁבִיעִי לְשֵׁשֶׁת יְמֵי הַמַּעֲשֶׂה. בֵּין קְדֻשַּׁת שַׁבָּת לִקְדֻשַּׁת יוֹם טוֹב הִבְדַּלְתָּ. וְאֶת יוֹם הַשְּׁבִיעִי מִשֵּׁשֶׁת יְמֵי הַמַּעֲשֶׂה קִדַּשְׁתָּ. הִבְדַּלְתָּ וְקִדַּשְׁתָּ אֶת עַמְּךָ יִשְׂרָאֵל בִּקְדֻשָּׁתֶךָ. בָּרוּךְ אַתָּה יְיָ, הַמַּבְדִּיל בֵּין קֹדֶשׁ לְקֹדֶשׁ:

Baruch atah, Ado-nai, Elo-haynoo, melech ha-olam, boray m'oray ha-aysh.

Baruch atah, Ado-nai, Elo-haynoo, melech ha-olam, ha-mavdil bayn ko-desh l'chol, bayn or l'choshech, bayn yisra-ayl la-amim, bayn yom ha-sh'vee-ee l'shayshet y'may ha-ma-aseh. Bayn k'dooshat shabbat li-k'dooshat yom tov hivdalta, v'et yom ha-sh'vee-ee mee-shayshet y'may ha-ma-aseh keedashta. Hivdalta v'keedashta et am'cha yisra-ayl bik'-doosha-techa. Baruch atah, Adonai, ha-mavdeel bayn ko-desh l'ko-desh.

Blessed are You, Lord, our God, King of the universe, Who created the lights of fire.

Blessed are you, Lord, our God, King of the universe, Who separated between holy and ordinary, between light and darkness, between Israel and the nations, and between the seventh day and the six work days. Between the sanctity of Shabbat and the sanctity of a festival You divided, and the seventh day from the six work days You sanctified. You have separated and sanctified Your people Israel with Your own holiness. Blessed are you, Lord, Who divided between holy and holy.

On all nights conclude here:

בָּרוּךְ אַתָּה יְיָ, אֱלֹהֵינוּ מֶלֶךְ הָעוֹלָם, שֶׁהֶחֱיָנוּ וְקִיְּמָנוּ וְהִגִּיעָנוּ לַזְּמַן הַזֶּה:

Baruch atah, Ado-nai, Elo-haynoo, melech ha-olam, she-he-che-yanoo, v'kee-y'manoo, v'heegee-anoo la-z'man ha-zeh.

Blessed are you, Lord, our God, King of the universe, Who has kept us alive, preserved us, and enabled us to reach this season.

Drink the first cup of wine while reclining on the left side.

12

The effect of wine–good wine–is that it lifts our spirits and helps us feel good. In Judaism, life and pleasure are synonymous. Even though the trials of life may obscure the pleasure of life's blessings, still, life is a pleasure. Wine in Jewish life is never used to drown out pain, but rather to assist us in reconnecting to the feeling that life is pleasurable.

On Passover we are lifted by the drinking of wine in two ways: (1) The redemption from Egypt took place a long time ago. Sometimes it is difficult to feel connected to these events and to the pleasure of being part of the Jewish nation. Wine helps. (2) Though the attainment of freedom may be cause for dancing in the streets, it also carries with it the burden of responsibility. This looming weight of accountability–the nuts and bolts of sovereignty–is enough to temper any celebration. So we drink a little wine–to lift us, and to remind us that, long after the headlines have faded, the deepest pleasure of freedom still remains–the pleasure of grabbing the reins of responsibility, of rolling up our sleeves and beginning to tackle all the many tasks necessary to transform promise into substance and dreams into reality.

❧ ורחץ ❧

Urechatz

Wash hands

Prepare a pitcher or large cup of water and a towel. We wash our hands, exactly as if we were washing before eating bread or matzah. However, we do not recite any blessing. In many homes, a basin and cup of water is passed around the table. The water is then poured over our right hand twice; we repeat the same process with the left hand. We then dry our hands with a towel.

❧ כרפס ❧

Karpas
Eat a vegetable dipped in salt water

Each seder participant dips a small piece of a vegetable (traditionally green pepper, celery, onions or a boiled potato) into a bowl of salt water.

Although many only use green vegetables, any vegetable upon which we recite the blessing of *Borei P'ri Ha-adamah*, "Who creates the fruit of the ground," may be used.

The seder leader dips a vegetable into salt water, and distributes small portions of it to all assembled. Before eating it, all recite the following blessing. When reciting the blessing, keep in mind the marror (bitter herbs), since this blessing applies also to the marror.

בָּרוּךְ אַתָּה יְיָ, אֱלֹהֵינוּ מֶלֶךְ הָעוֹלָם, בּוֹרֵא פְּרִי הָאֲדָמָה:

Baruch atah, Ado-nai, Elo-haynoo, melech ha-olam, boray p'ree ha-ada-mah.

Blessed are You, Lord, our God, King of the universe, Who created the fruit of the soil.

❧ *In ancient times, vegetables were served as appetizers, but only at the finest meals and banquets. On the night of Passover, every Jew is a member of an aristocratic family. We are people of status and wealth, as free as any king in his palace. We grace our seder plate with karpas, a venerable symbol of opulence, to express our sense that the feeling of being Jewish is the feeling of nobility.*

One of the main purposes of the seder and of reading the Haggadah is to interest children in the drama of Jewish history. There are even sections of the Haggadah involving children. In the Torah it is written, "You shall tell your son on that day, 'Because of this did the Almighty do for me when I went out of Egypt'" (Exodus 8:8). At the seder we want to provoke questions. We want the young people–and everyone else–at the seder to not merely *hear* the reading of the Haggadah, we want them to wonder about particular rituals.

"Why are we eating a vegetable dipped in salt water before the meal?" they may ask. Then we can answer, "A vegetable dipped in salt water could be an entire meal! A long time ago a slave would be grateful to receive some vegetables after a day of hard work! Even today, people in poor countries subsist on such simple fare!"

◈ יחץ ◈
Yachatz
Break the middle matzah

The middle matzah is broken and kept until after the meal is eaten when it is shared by everyone at the table.

This piece is called the Afikomen, and it is perhaps the most popular part of the seder for children. Each seder night a child searches out the Afikomen and hides it, holding it for "ransom" until the leader of the seder promises to give the child something in return.

The middle matzah is broken into two pieces. The smaller piece is placed between the other two matzot on the seder plate, and the larger piece is put away to be eaten later as the Afikomen.

In many ways children are the stars of the seder night. Jewish law states that the seder should begin as soon after nightfall as possible in order to make certain that all children, even the youngest, will be able to participate in as much of the seder as possible. Various customs, including spreading nuts or sweets on the table, exist specifically to arouse the curiosity of children and stimulate their active involvement. Likewise, the hiding and seeking of the Afikomen is one of the high points of the seder for most children. The annual Afikomen hunt has a way of transforming even the most bleary-eyed youngster into an exuberant seder enthusiast.

Like a child on the trail of the Afikomen, we too must see ourselves as seekers in life—seeking truth and meaning, for the kind of fulfillment that lasts longer than a week, and for riches that transcend the material. And, like children in search of the Afikomen, when focused on the urgency of our search for meaning, we will experience our efforts not only as the price of life but as its thrill and pleasure.

⋟ מַגִּיד ⋞

Maggid
Recite the Haggadah

In this unique ceremony, we read aloud from the Haggadah about Jewish suffering and growth. We recall the dramatic moment when the Jews left Egypt as slaves and became a free people, wandering for forty years in the desert before entering the promised land. We recount the many miracles that brought the Jews to freedom. And we express our appreciation to God Who liberated our ancestors from slavery and made us into a nation.

The optimum seder will include many generations, a sharing of histories, with room for everyone to contribute in the discussion of Jewish history and tradition. Younger members too will be brought into the recounting and learn about the meaning and depth of Jewish history and experience in their lives. The seder provides an opportunity to unite families in common history and ensure continuity in future generations.

The seder leader lifts the seder plate, uncovers the matzot, and all recite the following.

הָא לַחְמָא עַנְיָא דִּי אֲכָלוּ אַבְהָתָנָא בְּאַרְעָא דְמִצְרָיִם. כָּל דִּכְפִין יֵיתֵי
וְיֵכוֹל, כָּל דִּצְרִיךְ יֵיתֵי וְיִפְסַח. הָשַׁתָּא הָכָא, לְשָׁנָה הַבָּאָה בְּאַרְעָא
דְיִשְׂרָאֵל. הָשַׁתָּא עַבְדֵי, לְשָׁנָה הַבָּאָה בְּנֵי חוֹרִין:

Ha lachma anya dee achaloo avhatana b'ara d'mitzra-yim. Kol dich-fin yaytay v'yaychol. Kol ditz-rich yaytay v'yifsach. Hashata hacha. L'shana haba-ah b'arah d'yisra-ayl! Hashata av-day. L'shana haba-ah b'nay chorin!	*This is the poor bread that our forefathers ate in the land of Egypt. Let all who are hungry come and eat. Let all who are needy come and celebrate the Passover festival. Now we are here. Next year may we be in the land of Israel! Now we are slaves. Next year may we all be free!*

It's significant that the seder is begun in Aramaic, the common language of Jews when the Haggadah was composed. The seder thus calls upon *all* Jews to participate, even those who can do so only in English, today's common language.

⋟ *After uncovering the matzah–symbol of our physical deprivation–we immediately turn our thoughts to the needs of others. The Pharaohs and Hitlers of history have made countless attempts to demoralize us by first crushing our bodies, hoping that our spirits would then be easy prey. But we will not be subdued. Right from the outset of the seder we affirm our commitment to the maintenance of dignity despite all efforts by our oppressors to denude our hearts of human sentiment.*

In the Haggadah we are directed, "In each generation a Jew is obligated to view himself or herself as having gone out of Egypt." How is each of us supposed to feel as if we have personally left Egypt? One possibility is to try to empathize with the near-slavery we know still exists in the developing world, or with the dire poverty that people in our own cities often endure.

We can also, in a different sense, consider our own lack of freedom. The Hebrew for Egypt is *Mitzrayim*. The etymological root *tzar* means confined or stifled. Most of us experience a personal sense in which we are trapped, in which we live in our very own *Mitzrayim*. We may not have worked as slaves in the broiling heat of the desert, but true freedom is fleeting even today. We may be slaves to our mortgages, cars, or other material objects. Or we may be slaves to our bad habits. We may have never attained our full emotional, spiritual or psychological potential. Just spending this evening considering the whole notion of freedom can be instructive. Spiritually, we can always try to rise to higher levels, and recounting the struggles of yesterday can aid us in understanding and overcoming the struggles of today.

But this ruminating over our painful past should be joyful, since our physical enslavement is long over, and we are grateful for this. Our sense of joy this evening should be palpable. King Solomon composed a joyful book describing Israel's relationship to God and God's relationship to Israel. During the Shabbat of Passover, this book, *Song of Songs* (*Shir HaShirim*), is read. It contains a beautiful allegory that describes the love between God and the Jews.

One particular passage describes what God said to the Jews when He revealed that liberation from the suffering in Egypt was just around the corner, "My beloved raised his voice and said to me, 'Arise my beloved, my fair one, and come away. For behold, the winter has passed; the rain is over and gone. The blossoms have appeared in the land, the time of singing has arrived, and the voice of the turtledove is heard in our land.'"

The time of our bondage–which resembles winter–is over and we are a free people. For most of us in the Northern hemisphere, Passover occurs when renewal is all around us, with spring in the air. We can sense the imminent change. Passover provides the opportunity to consider our history–our transformation from penniless slaves into a free people–and evaluate the path on which we are now traveling.

Mah Nishtanah/The Four Questions

The *Mah Nishtanah* can actually be read in various ways. One can read it as four questions, as five questions, as one question with four examples or as one question with four answers. (Ask the people at your seder how many questions they see contained in the *Mah Nishtanah*.)

Regardless of how one understands the *Mah Nishtanah*, it is clearly calling our attention to a unique night. So we ask ourselves, why *is* this night different?

The matzot are covered again, and the seder plate is removed. The second cup of wine is now poured into everyone's cup. Now the youngest person present asks:

מַה נִּשְׁתַּנָּה הַלַּיְלָה הַזֶּה מִכָּל הַלֵּילוֹת?

שֶׁבְּכָל הַלֵּילוֹת אָנוּ אוֹכְלִין חָמֵץ וּמַצָּה. הַלַּיְלָה הַזֶּה כֻּלּוֹ מַצָּה:

שֶׁבְּכָל הַלֵּילוֹת אָנוּ אוֹכְלִין שְׁאָר יְרָקוֹת. הַלַּיְלָה הַזֶּה מָרוֹר:

שֶׁבְּכָל הַלֵּילוֹת אֵין אָנוּ מַטְבִּילִין אֲפִילוּ פַּעַם אֶחָת. הַלַּיְלָה הַזֶּה שְׁתֵּי פְעָמִים:

שֶׁבְּכָל הַלֵּילוֹת אָנוּ אוֹכְלִין בֵּין יוֹשְׁבִין וּבֵין מְסֻבִּין. הַלַּיְלָה הַזֶּה כֻּלָּנוּ מְסֻבִּין:

Mah nishtanah ha-lailah ha-zeh meekol ha-laylot?

Sheb'chol ha-laylot, a-noo och'lin chamaytz oo-matzah, ha-laila ha-zeh koolo matzah.

Sheb'chol ha-laylot, a-noo och'lin sh'ar y'rakot, ha-laila ha-zeh marror.

Sheb'chol ha-laylot, ayn a-noo matbeelin afee-loo pa-am echat, ha-laila ha-zeh sh'tay f'amim.

Sheb'chol ha-laylot, a-noo och'lin bayn yosh'vin oovayn m'soobin, ha-laila ha-zeh koo-lanoo m'soobin.

Why is this night different from all other nights?

On all other nights, we eat both bread and matzah, but on this night only matzah.

On all other nights, we eat all types of herbs, but on this night we eat marror (bitter herbs).

On all other nights, we do not dip even once, but on this night we dip twice.

On all other nights, we eat either sitting or reclining, but on this night we all recline.

18

The enslavement mentioned in "*Avadim Hayinu…*" alludes to the multiple meanings of slavery. Furthermore, just as slavery has connotations beyond physical bondage, so the reference to Egypt is more than just geographic.

The Hebrew word for Egypt, *Mitzrayim*, signifies constraint, the feeling of being stifled. A slave is certainly constrained and stifled. And aren't we all? Can't we all admit to ourselves that there are aspects of our lives that seem to be beyond our control—or anyone else's? That no matter how desperately we want something, we can't seem to discipline ourselves in ways that will facilitate achievement? That no matter how hard we try, we keep making the same mistakes over and over again? Well, how about this for a radical idea—ask God for help! It's not like He took early retirement after the exodus from Egypt, you know.

If an atheist in a foxhole will always turn to God for help, why can't we? Perhaps you could say that another way to translate *Mitzrayim* is a foxhole, and as we know, life is full of little foxholes.

The matzot are now uncovered, and the seder leader replies, accompanied by the entire assembly:

עֲבָדִים הָיִינוּ לְפַרְעֹה בְּמִצְרָיִם. וַיּוֹצִיאֵנוּ יְיָ אֱלֹהֵינוּ מִשָּׁם, בְּיָד חֲזָקָה
וּבִזְרוֹעַ נְטוּיָה, וְאִלּוּ לֹא הוֹצִיא הַקָּדוֹשׁ בָּרוּךְ הוּא אֶת־אֲבוֹתֵינוּ
מִמִּצְרַיִם, הֲרֵי אָנוּ וּבָנֵינוּ וּבְנֵי בָנֵינוּ, מְשֻׁעְבָּדִים הָיִינוּ לְפַרְעֹה
בְּמִצְרָיִם. וַאֲפִילוּ כֻּלָּנוּ חֲכָמִים, כֻּלָּנוּ נְבוֹנִים, כֻּלָּנוּ זְקֵנִים, כֻּלָּנוּ
יוֹדְעִים אֶת־הַתּוֹרָה, מִצְוָה עָלֵינוּ לְסַפֵּר בִּיצִיאַת מִצְרָיִם. וְכָל הַמַּרְבֶּה
לְסַפֵּר בִּיצִיאַת מִצְרָיִם, הֲרֵי זֶה מְשֻׁבָּח:

Ava-dim ha-yeenoo l'pharo b'mitzra-yim, va-yotzee-aynoo Adonai Elo-haynoo meesham b'yad chaza-kah oovizro-ah n'too-yah. V'ee-loo lo hotzee ha-kadosh, baruch hoo, et avotaynoo mee-mitzra-yim, ha-ray a-noo, oo-va-naynoo, oov'nay va-naynoo m'shoo-badim ha-yeenoo l'pharo b'mitzro-yim. Va-afee-loo koo-lanoo

We were slaves to Pharaoh in Egypt, and the Lord, our God took us out of there with a mighty hand and an outstretched arm. And if the Holy One, blessed be He, had not taken our fathers out of Egypt, then we, our children, and our children's children would still be enslaved to Pharaoh in Egypt. And even if we were all wise, all full of understanding, all advanced in years, all

chachamim, koo-lanoo n'vonim, koo-lanoo z'kaynim, koo-lanoo yod'im et ha-torah, mitzvah a-laynoo l'sapayr beetzee-at mitzra-yim. V'chol ha-marbeh l'sapayr beetzee-at mitzra-yim, ha-ray zeh m'shoobach.

knowledgeable of the Torah, it is still incumbent upon us to tell about the Exodus from Egypt. And the more one tells of the Exodus from Egypt, the more praiseworthy one is.

מַעֲשֶׂה בְּרַבִּי אֱלִיעֶזֶר, וְרַבִּי יְהוֹשֻׁעַ, וְרַבִּי אֶלְעָזָר בֶּן־עֲזַרְיָה, וְרַבִּי עֲקִיבָא, וְרַבִּי טַרְפוֹן, שֶׁהָיוּ מְסֻבִּין בִּבְנֵי־בְרַק, וְהָיוּ מְסַפְּרִים בִּיצִיאַת מִצְרַיִם, כָּל־אוֹתוֹ הַלַּיְלָה, עַד שֶׁבָּאוּ תַלְמִידֵיהֶם וְאָמְרוּ לָהֶם: רַבּוֹתֵינוּ, הִגִּיעַ זְמַן קְרִיאַת שְׁמַע, שֶׁל שַׁחֲרִית:

Ma-aseh b'ra-bee Elee-ezer, v'ra-bee Y'hoshoo-ah, v'rabee Elazar ben Azaryah, v'ra-bee Akeevah, v'ra-bee Tarfon she-ha-yoo m'soobin biv'nay v'rak. V'ha-yoo m'saprim beetzee-at mitzra-yim kol oto ha-lailah, ad she-ba-oo talmeeday-hem v'am'roo la-hem, Rabotaynoo, heegee-ah z'man k'ree-at sh'ma shel shacharit.

It is told that Rabbi Eliezer, Rabbi Joshua, Rabbi Elazar Ben Azariah, Rabbi Akiva, and Rabbi Tarfon were reclining together at a seder in Bnei Brak. They spoke of the Exodus from Egypt throughout the night, until their disciples came and said to them, "Our Masters, it is time to recite the morning Shema."

אָמַר רַבִּי אֶלְעָזָר בֶּן־עֲזַרְיָה. הֲרֵי אֲנִי כְּבֶן שִׁבְעִים שָׁנָה, וְלֹא זָכִיתִי, שֶׁתֵּאָמֵר יְצִיאַת מִצְרַיִם בַּלֵּילוֹת. עַד שֶׁדְּרָשָׁהּ בֶּן זוֹמָא. שֶׁנֶּאֱמַר: לְמַעַן תִּזְכֹּר, אֶת יוֹם צֵאתְךָ מֵאֶרֶץ מִצְרַיִם, כֹּל יְמֵי חַיֶּיךָ. יְמֵי חַיֶּיךָ הַיָּמִים. כֹּל יְמֵי חַיֶּיךָ הַלֵּילוֹת. וַחֲכָמִים אוֹמְרִים: יְמֵי חַיֶּיךָ הָעוֹלָם הַזֶּה. כֹּל יְמֵי חַיֶּיךָ לְהָבִיא לִימוֹת הַמָּשִׁיחַ:

Amar ra-bee Elazar ben Azaryah: Ha-ray a-nee k'ven shivim shana, v'lo zacheetee shetay-amayr y'tzee-at mitzra-yim ba-laylot, ad shed'rasha Ben Zoma. She-ne-emar, l'ma-an tizkor et yom tzayt-cha may-eretz mitzra-yim kol y'may cha-yecha.

Rabbi Elazar Ben Azariah said: "I am like a man of seventy, yet I have never suc-ceeded in proving that the Exodus from Egypt should be mentioned at night, until Ben Zoma explained it. For it is written, 'That you should remember the day you came forth from Egypt all the days of your

Y'may cha-yecha, ha-yamim. Kol y'may cha-yecha, ha-laylot. Va-cha-chamim om'rim, y'may cha-yecha, ha-olam hazeh. Kol y'may cha-yecha, l'ha-vee leemot ha-mashee-ach.

life' (Deut. 16:3). 'The days of your life" implies that we must mention it only during the days. 'All the days of your life,' however, includes the nights as well. The Sages, however, explain that 'the days of your life' implies that we must mention the Exodus only in the present world. 'All the days of your life' refers to the time of the Messiah as well."

בָּרוּךְ הַמָּקוֹם. בָּרוּךְ הוּא. בָּרוּךְ שֶׁנָּתַן תּוֹרָה לְעַמּוֹ יִשְׂרָאֵל. בָּרוּךְ הוּא כְּנֶגֶד אַרְבָּעָה בָנִים דִּבְּרָה תוֹרָה. אֶחָד חָכָם, וְאֶחָד רָשָׁע, וְאֶחָד תָּם, וְאֶחָד שֶׁאֵינוֹ יוֹדֵעַ לִשְׁאוֹל:

Baruch ha-makom, baruch hoo. Baruch she-natan Torah l'-a-mo yisra-ayl, baruch hoo. K'neged arba-ah ba-nim dib'rah Torah: Echad chacham, v'echad rasha, v'echad tam, v'echad she-ayno yoday-a lishol.

Blessed be the Ever-Present, blessed be He. Blessed be He who gave the Torah to His people Israel, blessed be He.

The Torah speaks of four sons: one wise, one wicked, one simple, and one who does not know how to ask.

חָכָם מַה הוּא אוֹמֵר? מָה הָעֵדֹת וְהַחֻקִּים וְהַמִּשְׁפָּטִים, אֲשֶׁר צִוָּה יְיָ אֱלֹהֵינוּ אֶתְכֶם? וְאַף אַתָּה אֱמָר-לוֹ כְּהִלְכוֹת הַפֶּסַח: אֵין מַפְטִירִין אַחַר הַפֶּסַח אֲפִיקוֹמָן:

Chacham, mah hoo omayr? Mah ha-aydot, v'ha-chookim, v'ha-mish-pa-tim, asher tzeevah Ado-nai, Elo-haynoo, et-chem? V'af atah emar lo k'hil'chot ha-pesach–Ayn maf-tee-rin achar ha-pesach afeekoman.

The wise son, what does he say? "What are the testimonies, the laws, and the ordinances that the Lord, our God, has commanded you?" Tell him of all the laws of Passover–including that one may not eat any dessert after the Paschal offering.

רָשָׁע מַה הוּא אוֹמֵר? מָה הָעֲבֹדָה הַזֹּאת לָכֶם? לָכֶם וְלֹא לוֹ. וּלְפִי שֶׁהוֹצִיא אֶת-עַצְמוֹ מִן הַכְּלָל, כָּפַר בָּעִקָּר. וְאַף אַתָּה הַקְהֵה אֶת-שִׁנָּיו, וְאֱמָר-לוֹ: בַּעֲבוּר זֶה, עָשָׂה יְיָ לִי, בְּצֵאתִי מִמִּצְרָיִם, לִי וְלֹא-לוֹ. אִלּוּ הָיָה שָׁם, לֹא הָיָה נִגְאָל:

Rasha, mah hoo omayr? Mah ha-avodah ha-zot la-chem? La-chem, v'lo lo. Oo-l'fee she-hotzee et atzmo min ha-k'lal, kafar b'-ee-kar. V'af atah hak-hay et sheenav, ve-emar lo, ba-avoor zeh asah Ado-nai lee b'tzaytee meemitzra-yim. Lee, v'lo lo. Ee-loo ha-yah sham, lo ha-yah nig-al.

The wicked son, what does he say? "What is this service to you?" By saying "to you" he excludes himself from the community. By excluding himself, he has denied a fundamental principle of our faith. Therefore, you must cause him distress, by stating, "Because of this, the Lord did this for me when I came out of Egypt." For me, but not for him. Had he been there, he would not have been redeemed.

תָּם מַה הוּא אוֹמֵר? מַה זֹּאת? וְאָמַרְתָּ אֵלָיו: בְּחֹזֶק יָד הוֹצִיאָנוּ יְיָ מִמִּצְרַיִם מִבֵּית עֲבָדִים:

If we ever stop marveling at life's questions, if we temper our single-minded pursuit of answers, we will never succeed at attaining wisdom. In fact, the question here, "What is this?"—referring to the search for answers, whatever our level of intelligence—is not such a simple question after all.

Tam, mah hoo omayr? Mah zot? V'amarta aylav, b'chozek yad hotzee-anoo Ado-nai meemitzra-yim, meebayt avadim.

The simple son, what does he say? He says "What is this?" You should say to him, "With a mighty hand did the Lord take us out of Egypt, out of the house of bondage."

וְשֶׁאֵינוֹ יוֹדֵעַ לִשְׁאוֹל, אַתְּ פְּתַח לוֹ. שֶׁנֶּאֱמַר: וְהִגַּדְתָּ לְבִנְךָ, בַּיּוֹם הַהוּא לֵאמֹר: בַּעֲבוּר זֶה עָשָׂה יְיָ לִי, בְּצֵאתִי מִמִּצְרָיִם:

V'she-ayno yoday-a lishol, at p'tach lo. She-ne-emar, V'hee-gad'ta l'vin'cha ba-yom ha-hoo, laymor: Ba-avoor zeh, asah Ado-nai lee b'tzaytee meemitzra-yim.

As for the son who does not know how to ask, you should initiate the discussion with him, as it is stated, "And you should tell your child on that day, saying: 'Because of this, the Lord did this did for me when I came out of Egypt.'"

יָכוֹל מֵרֹאשׁ חֹדֶשׁ, תַּלְמוּד לוֹמַר בַּיּוֹם הַהוּא. אִי בַּיּוֹם הַהוּא. יָכוֹל מִבְּעוֹד יוֹם. תַּלְמוּד לוֹמַר, בַּעֲבוּר זֶה. בַּעֲבוּר זֶה לֹא אָמַרְתִּי, אֶלָּא בְּשָׁעָה שֶׁיֵּשׁ מַצָּה וּמָרוֹר מֻנָּחִים לְפָנֶיךָ:

Yachol may-rosh chodesh. Talmud lomar, ba-yom ha-hoo. Ee ba-yom ha-hoo, Yachol mee-b'od yom. Talmud lomar, Ba-avoor zeh.

One might think that the duty to discuss the Exodus begins on the new moon of Nissan. The Torah, therefore, says "on that day." The expression "on that day" suggests

Ba-avoor zeh lo amartee ela b'sha-ah she-yaysh matzah oo-maror moonachim l'fa-necha.

that this discussion should take place in the daytime; therefore, the Torah says "because of this" which implies that the discussion should take place only when matzah and bitter herbs are placed before you.

מִתְּחִלָּה עוֹבְדֵי עֲבוֹדָה זָרָה הָיוּ אֲבוֹתֵינוּ. וְעַכְשָׁו קֵרְבָנוּ הַמָּקוֹם לַעֲבוֹדָתוֹ. שֶׁנֶּאֱמַר: וַיֹּאמֶר יְהוֹשֻׁעַ אֶל־כָּל־הָעָם. כֹּה אָמַר יְיָ אֱלֹהֵי יִשְׂרָאֵל, בְּעֵבֶר הַנָּהָר יָשְׁבוּ אֲבוֹתֵיכֶם מֵעוֹלָם, תֶּרַח אֲבִי אַבְרָהָם וַאֲבִי נָחוֹר. וַיַּעַבְדוּ אֱלֹהִים אֲחֵרִים: וָאֶקַּח אֶת־אֲבִיכֶם אֶת־אַבְרָהָם מֵעֵבֶר הַנָּהָר, וָאוֹלֵךְ אוֹתוֹ בְּכָל־אֶרֶץ כְּנָעַן. וָאַרְבֶּה אֶת־זַרְעוֹ, וָאֶתֶּן לוֹ אֶת־יִצְחָק: וָאֶתֵּן לְיִצְחָק אֶת־יַעֲקֹב וְאֶת־עֵשָׂו. וָאֶתֵּן לְעֵשָׂו אֶת־הַר שֵׂעִיר, לָרֶשֶׁת אוֹתוֹ. וְיַעֲקֹב וּבָנָיו יָרְדוּ מִצְרָיִם:

Mee-t'cheelah, ov'day avodah zarah ha-yoo avotaynoo. V'ach-shav kayr'-vaynoo ha-makom la-avodato, she-ne-emar, Va-yo-mer Y'ho-shoo-a el kol ha-am: Ko amar Ado-nai Elo-hay yisra-ayl, b'ayver ha-na-har yashvoo avotay-chem may-olam, Terach, avee Avraham, va-avee Nachor; va-ya-av-doo elo-him achayrim. Va-ekach et aveechem et Avraham may-ayver ha-na-har, va-olaych oto b'chol eretz k'na-an, va-arbeh et zaro va-eten lo et Yitz-chak. Va-etayn l'Yitz-chak et Ya-akov v'et Aysav. Va-etayn l'Aysav et har sayeer la-reshet oto, v'Ya-akov oo-vanav yardoo mitzra-yim.

In the beginning, our fathers were idol worshipers. Now God has brought us near to His service, as it is written, "And Joshua said to the whole nation: 'Thus said the Lord God of Israel, Your fathers dwelt on the other side of the river from earliest time, Terach, the father of Abraham, and the father of Nachor; and they served other gods. And I took your father Abraham from the other side of the river, and I led him throughout all of the land of Canaan, and I multiplied his seed and gave him Isaac. And to Isaac I gave Jacob and Esau. To Esau I gave Mount Seir to inherit it, but Jacob and his children went down into Egypt'" (Josh. 24:2-4).

When the Haggadah says that Abraham "dwelt on the other side of the river," it means that he, the first Jew, was different from everyone else in the world. One of the toughest things in life is to be different from others, but we all contain within ourselves the strength to withstand such trials. We just have to trust in our own strength.

בָּרוּךְ שׁוֹמֵר הַבְטָחָתוֹ לְיִשְׂרָאֵל. בָּרוּךְ הוּא. שֶׁהַקָּדוֹשׁ בָּרוּךְ הוּא חִשַּׁב אֶת־הַקֵּץ, לַעֲשׂוֹת כְּמָה שֶׁאָמַר לְאַבְרָהָם אָבִינוּ בִּבְרִית בֵּין הַבְּתָרִים, שֶׁנֶּאֱמַר: וַיֹּאמֶר לְאַבְרָם יָדֹעַ תֵּדַע, כִּי־גֵר יִהְיֶה זַרְעֲךָ,

בְּאֶרֶץ לֹא לָהֶם, וַעֲבָדוּם וְעִנּוּ אֹתָם אַרְבַּע מֵאוֹת שָׁנָה: וְגַם אֶת־הַגּוֹי אֲשֶׁר יַעֲבֹדוּ דָּן אָנֹכִי. וְאַחֲרֵי כֵן יֵצְאוּ, בִּרְכֻשׁ גָּדוֹל:

Baruch shomayr havta-cha-to l'-yisra-ayl; baruch hoo! She-ha-kadosh, baruch hoo, chee-shav et ha-kaytz la-asot k'mah she-amar l'Avraham avee-noo biv-rit bayn ha-b'ta-rim, she-ne-emar, Va-yo-mer l'Avram: Yado-a tay-da kee gayr yee-h'yeh zar-acha b'eretz lo la-hem; va-ava-doom v'ee-noo otam arba mayot shanah. V'gam et ha-goy asher ya-avo-doo dan ano-chee, v'acharay chayn yaytz'oo bir-chush ga-dol.	*Blessed is He who keeps His promise to Israel; Blessed is He! For the Holy One, blessed is He, determined the end of the bondage in order to fulfill His promise to Abraham our father in the covenant between the parts, as it is stated, "And He said to Abram: You should surely know that your seed will be strangers in a land not theirs; they will enslave them and oppress them for four hundred years. But also the nation that they will serve will I judge, and afterward they shall go forth with great wealth" (Gen. 15:13-14).*

We lift our cup of wine, cover the matzot and recite:

וְהִיא שֶׁעָמְדָה לַאֲבוֹתֵינוּ וְלָנוּ. שֶׁלֹּא אֶחָד בִּלְבַד, עָמַד עָלֵינוּ לְכַלּוֹתֵנוּ. אֶלָּא שֶׁבְּכָל דּוֹר וָדוֹר, עוֹמְדִים עָלֵינוּ לְכַלּוֹתֵנוּ. וְהַקָּדוֹשׁ בָּרוּךְ הוּא מַצִּילֵנוּ מִיָּדָם:

V'hee she-am'dah la-avotaynoo v'la-noo. Shelo echod bil'vad amad a-laynoo l'cha-lotaynoo, ela sheb'-chol dor va-dor om'dim a-laynoo l'cha-lotaynoo; v'ha-kadosh, baruch hoo, mahtzee-laynoo mee-yadam.	*It is this promise that has sustained our fathers and us. For not only one persecutor has risen up against us to destroy us, but in every generation they rise up against us to destroy us; but the Holy One, blessed is He, delivers us from their hands.*

We lower the wine and uncover the matzot.

צֵא וּלְמַד, מַה בִּקֵּשׁ לָבָן הָאֲרַמִּי לַעֲשׂוֹת לְיַעֲקֹב אָבִינוּ. שֶׁפַּרְעֹה לֹא גָזַר אֶלָּא עַל הַזְּכָרִים, וְלָבָן בִּקֵּשׁ לַעֲקֹר אֶת־הַכֹּל, שֶׁנֶּאֱמַר: אֲרַמִּי אֹבֵד אָבִי, וַיֵּרֶד מִצְרַיְמָה, וַיָּגָר שָׁם בִּמְתֵי מְעָט. וַיְהִי שָׁם לְגוֹי גָּדוֹל, עָצוּם וָרָב:

Tzay oo-l'mahd mah beekaysh Lavan ha-ara-mee la-asot l'Ya-akov avee-noo. She-Paroh lo ga-zar ela al ha-z'charim, v'Lavan beekaysh la-akor et ha-kol. She-ne-emar, Ara-mee ovayd a-vee, va-yay-red mitz-rai-mah va-ya-gar sham, bim'-tay m'at, va-y'hee sham l'goy ga-dol, a-tzoom va-rav.

Go out and learn what Laban the Aramean sought to do to Jacob our father. Whereas Pharaoh decreed death only upon the males, Laban sought to uproot all. As it is stated, "An Aramean sought to destroy my father, and he went down to Egypt and sojourned there as a stranger, few in number, and there he became a great nation, strong and numerous" (Deut. 26:5).

וַיֵּרֶד מִצְרַיְמָה, אָנוּס עַל פִּי הַדִּבּוּר. וַיָּגָר שָׁם. מְלַמֵּד שֶׁלֹא יָרַד יַעֲקֹב אָבִינוּ לְהִשְׁתַּקֵּעַ בְּמִצְרַיִם, אֶלָּא לָגוּר שָׁם, שֶׁנֶּאֱמַר: וַיֹּאמְרוּ אֶל־פַּרְעֹה, לָגוּר בָּאָרֶץ בָּאנוּ, כִּי אֵין מִרְעֶה לַצֹּאן אֲשֶׁר לַעֲבָדֶיךָ, כִּי כָבֵד הָרָעָב בְּאֶרֶץ כְּנָעַן. וְעַתָּה, יֵשְׁבוּ־נָא עֲבָדֶיךָ בְּאֶרֶץ גֹּשֶׁן:

Va-yay-red mitz-rai-mah – a-noos ahl pee ha-deeboor. Va-ya-gar sham – m'la-mayd shelo ya-rad Ya-akov avee-noo l'hishta-kay-a b'mitzra-yim ela la-goor sham. She-ne-emar, Va-yom'roo el Paroh, la-goor ba-a-retz ba-noo, kee ayn mi-reh la-tzon asher la-ava-decha, kee cha-vayd ha-ra-av b'eretz k'na-an, V'atah, yaysh'voo na ava-decha b'eretz Goshen.

"And he went down to Egypt"– compelled by the divine decree.

"And sojourned there"–This teaches us that he did not go down to settle in Egypt but only to sojourn there. As it is stated, "And Jacob's sons said to Pharaoh, 'We have come to sojourn in the land, for your servants' flocks have no pasture, for the famine is severe in the land of Canaan. Now, please let your servants dwell in the land of Goshen'" (Gen. 47:4).

בִּמְתֵי מְעָט. כְּמָה שֶׁנֶּאֱמַר: בְּשִׁבְעִים נֶפֶשׁ, יָרְדוּ אֲבֹתֶיךָ מִצְרַיְמָה. וְעַתָּה, שָׂמְךָ יְיָ אֱלֹהֶיךָ, כְּכוֹכְבֵי הַשָּׁמַיִם לָרֹב.

Bim'tay m'aht – k'mah she-ne-emar, b'shivim nefesh yar'doo avo-techa mitz-rai-mah. V'atah sam'cha Ado-nai Elo-hecha k'choch'vay ha-sha-mayim la-rov.

"Few in number"–as it is stated, "With seventy souls your fathers went down to Egypt. Now the Lord your God has made you like the stars of heaven for multitude" (Deut. 10:22).

❧ "Forced by the decree of God…" We often have little contol over the circumstances of our lives and the situations with which we are confronted. There is Divine orchestration in life. Our role–our shot at freedom– is to address the conditions of our lives and to respond to all that comes our way with the dignity, maturity, and courage that transforms us into better human beings.

וַיְהִי שָׁם לְגוֹי. מְלַמֵּד שֶׁהָיוּ יִשְׂרָאֵל מְצֻיָּנִים שָׁם:

Vay'hee sham l'goy – m'la-mayd she-hayoo yisra-ayl m'tzoo-yanim sham.

"And there he became a great nation"– This teaches us that Israel was distinguished there.

גָּדוֹל עָצוּם, כְּמָה שֶׁנֶּאֱמַר: וּבְנֵי יִשְׂרָאֵל, פָּרוּ וַיִּשְׁרְצוּ, וַיִּרְבּוּ וַיַּעַצְמוּ, בִּמְאֹד מְאֹד, וַתִּמָּלֵא הָאָרֶץ אֹתָם:

Gadol a-tzoom – k'mah she-ne-emar, Oo-v'nay yisra-ayl pa-roo va-yish-r'tzoo va-yirboo va-ya-atz'moo bim'od m'od, va-tee-ma-lay ha-aretz otam.

"Strong"–as it is stated, "The children of Israel were fruitful and swarmed and increased and became very very strong, and the land became filled with them" (Ex. 1:7).

וָרָב. כְּמָה שֶׁנֶּאֱמַר: רְבָבָה כְּצֶמַח הַשָּׂדֶה נְתַתִּיךְ, וַתִּרְבִּי, וַתִּגְדְּלִי, וַתָּבֹאִי בַּעֲדִי עֲדָיִים: שָׁדַיִם נָכֹנוּ, וּשְׂעָרֵךְ צִמֵּחַ, וְאַתְּ עֵרֹם וְעֶרְיָה:

Varav – k'mah she-ne-emar, R'vavah, k'tzemach ha-sa-deh n'ta-teecha, va-teerbee va-tig-d'lee, va-tavo-ee ba-adee ada-yim, sha-dai-im na-cho-noo oo-s'a-raych tzeemay-ach, v'at ayrom v'er-yah.

"Numerous"–as it is stated, "Myriads, like the plants of the field I have made you, and you have increased and grown, and you come with perfect beauty, breasts fashioned and your hair grown, but you were naked and bare" (Ezek. 16:7).

וָאֶעֱבֹר עָלַיִךְ וָאֶרְאֵךְ מִתְבּוֹסֶסֶת בְּדָמָיִךְ וָאֹמַר לָךְ בְּדָמַיִךְ חֲיִי וָאֹמַר לָךְ בְּדָמַיִךְ חֲיִי.

Va-eh-evor ala-yich, va-er-aych mit-bo-seset b'dama-yich, va-omar lach: B'dama-yich cha-yee! Va-omar lach: B'dama-yich cha-yee!

I passed over you, saw you downtrodden in your blood, and said to you: "Through your blood you shall live!" And I said to you: "Through your blood you shall live!"

וַיָּרֵעוּ אֹתָנוּ הַמִּצְרִים וַיְעַנּוּנוּ. וַיִּתְּנוּ עָלֵינוּ עֲבֹדָה קָשָׁה: וַיָּרֵעוּ אֹתָנוּ הַמִּצְרִים. כְּמָה שֶׁנֶּאֱמַר: הָבָה נִתְחַכְּמָה לוֹ. פֶּן־יִרְבֶּה, וְהָיָה כִּי־תִקְרֶאנָה מִלְחָמָה, וְנוֹסַף גַּם הוּא עַל־שֹׂנְאֵינוּ, וְנִלְחַם־בָּנוּ וְעָלָה מִן־הָאָרֶץ:

Va-ya-rayoo otanoo ha-mitzrim va-y'a-noonoo va-yit'noo a-laynoo avodah ka-shah. Va-ya-rayoo otanoo ha-mitzrim–k'mah she-ne-emar, Ha-vah, nit-chak'mah lo, pen yirbeh, v'ha-yah kee tikrenah mil-chamah, v'nosaf gam hoo al so-n'aynoo v'nil-cham ba-noo v'alah min ha-aretz.

"And the Egyptians mistreated us and afflicted us and imposed hard labor upon us" (Deut. 26:6). "And the Egyptians mis-treated us"–as it is stated, "Come, let us deal shrewdly with them, lest they increase, and if a war befalls us, they will join our enemies and fight against us and leave the land" (Ex. 1:10).

וַיְעַנּוּנוּ. כְּמָה שֶׁנֶּאֱמַר: וַיָּשִׂימוּ עָלָיו שָׂרֵי מִסִּים, לְמַעַן עַנֹּתוֹ בְּסִבְלֹתָם: וַיִּבֶן עָרֵי מִסְכְּנוֹת לְפַרְעֹה, אֶת־פִּתֹם וְאֶת־רַעַמְסֵס: וַיִּתְּנוּ עָלֵינוּ עֲבֹדָה קָשָׁה. כְּמָה שֶׁנֶּאֱמַר: וַיַּעֲבִדוּ מִצְרַיִם אֶת־בְּנֵי יִשְׂרָאֵל בְּפָרֶךְ:

Va-y'a-noonoo – k'mah she-ne-emar, Va-ya-seemoo alav sa-ray mee-sim l'ma-an anoto b'siv'lotam, va-yee-ven ah-ray misk'not l'Pharoh, et pitom v'et ra-am-sayss. Va-yitnoo ah-laynoo avodah ka-shah – k'mah she-ne-emar, Va-ya-ahveedoo mitzra-yim et b'nay yisra-ayl b'farech.

"And afflicted us"–as it is stated, "They appointed over them taskmasters to afflict them with their burdens, and they built store cities for Pharaoh, Pithom and Raamses" (Ex. 1:11). "And imposed hard labor upon us"–as it is stated, "The Egyptians enslaved the children of Israel with back-breaking labor" (Ex. 1:13).

וַנִּצְעַק אֶל־יְיָ אֱלֹהֵי אֲבֹתֵינוּ, וַיִּשְׁמַע יְיָ אֶת־קֹלֵנוּ, וַיַּרְא אֶת־עָנְיֵנוּ, וְאֶת־עֲמָלֵנוּ, וְאֶת לַחֲצֵנוּ: וַנִּצְעַק אֶל־יְיָ אֱלֹהֵי אֲבֹתֵינוּ, כְּמָה שֶׁנֶּאֱמַר: וַיְהִי בַיָּמִים הָרַבִּים הָהֵם, וַיָּמָת מֶלֶךְ מִצְרַיִם, וַיֵּאָנְחוּ בְנֵי־יִשְׂרָאֵל מִן־הָעֲבֹדָה וַיִּזְעָקוּ. וַתַּעַל שַׁוְעָתָם אֶל־הָאֱלֹהִים מִן־הָעֲבֹדָה:

Va-nitzak el Ado-nai, Elo-hay avotaynoo, va-yishma Ado-nai et kolaynoo va-yar et an-yay-noo, v'et ama-laynoo, v'et lacha-tzaynoo.

Va-nitzak el Ado-nai, Elo-hay avotaynoo – k'mah she-ne-emar, Va-y'hee va-ya-mim ha-ra-bim ha-haym va-ya-mat melech mitzra-yim, va-yay-an'choo v'nay yisra-ayl min

"And we cried out to the Lord, the God of our fathers, and the Lord heard our voice and saw our affliction, our toil, and our oppression" (Deut. 26:7).

"And we cried out to the Lord, the God of our fathers"–as it is stated, "It came to pass in those many days that the king of Egypt died, and the children of Israel sighed from the labor, and they cried out,

Pharaoh chose the site of Pithom and Raamses–a wet, sandy marshland–because he hoped that the futility of the Jew's efforts would give rise to a sense of inescapable anguish and despair. Each morning, the Jews were once again saddled with the burden of their fruitless and meaningless task. Part of the responsibility of freedom is the obligation to fill our lives with meaning. In a world filled with a thousand follies masquerading as life's most cherished activities, that responsibility weighs particularly heavy.

ha-avodah, va-yizakoo, va-ta-al shav-
atam el ha-Elo-him min ha-avodah.

and their cry ascended to God from the labor" (Ex. 2:23).

וַיִּשְׁמַע יְיָ אֶת־קֹלֵנוּ. כְּמָה שֶׁנֶּאֱמַר: וַיִּשְׁמַע אֱלֹהִים אֶת־נַאֲקָתָם,
וַיִּזְכֹּר אֱלֹהִים אֶת־בְּרִיתוֹ, אֶת־אַבְרָהָם, אֶת־יִצְחָק, וְאֶת יַעֲקֹב:

Va-yishmah Ado-nai et kolaynoo
– k'mah she-ne-emar, Va-yishmah
Elo-him et na-aka-tam, va-yizkor
Elo-him et b'ree-to et Avraham, et
Yitzchak, v'et Ya-akov.

"And the Lord heard our voice"—as it is stated, "God heard their cry, and God remembered His covenant with Abraham, with Isaac, and with Jacob" (Ex. 2:24).

וַיַּרְא אֶת־עָנְיֵנוּ: זוֹ פְּרִישׁוּת דֶּרֶךְ אֶרֶץ. כְּמָה שֶׁנֶּאֱמַר: וַיַּרְא אֱלֹהִים
אֶת־בְּנֵי יִשְׂרָאֵל. וַיֵּדַע אֱלֹהִים:

Va-yar et an-yaynoo – zo preeshut
derech eretz, k'mah she-ne-emar,
Va-yar Elo-him et b'nay yisra-ayl,
va-yaydah Elo-him.

"And saw our affliction"—This refers to the separation of a man from his wife, as it is stated, "And God saw the children of Israel, and God knew" (Ex. 2:24).

וְאֶת־עֲמָלֵנוּ. אֵלּוּ הַבָּנִים. כְּמָה שֶׁנֶּאֱמַר: כָּל־הַבֵּן הַיִּלּוֹד הַיְאֹרָה
תַּשְׁלִיכֻהוּ, וְכָל־הַבַּת תְּחַיּוּן:

V'et ama-laynoo– ayloo ha-
banim, k'mah she-ne-emar, Kol ha-
ben ha-yeelod ha-y'orah tashlee-
choo-hoo, v'chol ha-bat t'cha-yoon.

"Our toil"—This refers to the sons, as it is stated, "Every son who is born you shall cast into the Nile, and every daughter you shall allow to live" (Ex. 1:22).

וְאֶת לַחֲצֵנוּ. זוֹ הַדְּחַק. כְּמָה שֶׁנֶּאֱמַר: וְגַם־רָאִיתִי אֶת־הַלַּחַץ, אֲשֶׁר
מִצְרַיִם לֹחֲצִים אֹתָם:

V'et la-chatzaynoo – zo ha-d'chak,
k'mah she-ne-emar, V'gam ra-eetee
et ha-lachatz asher mitzra-yim
lochatzim otam.

"And our oppression"—This refers to the pressure of their hard work, as it is stated, "and I have also seen the oppression that the Egyptians are oppressing them" (Ex. 3:9).

וַיּוֹצִאֵנוּ יְיָ מִמִּצְרַיִם, בְּיָד חֲזָקָה, וּבִזְרֹעַ נְטוּיָה, וּבְמֹרָא גָדֹל וּבְאֹתוֹת וּבְמֹפְתִים:

Va-yotzee-aynoo Ado-nai mee-mitzra-yim b'yad chaza-kah, oo-viz'ro-a n'too-yah, oo-v'mora ga-dol, oo-v'otot oo-v'mof'tim.

"And the Lord took us out of Egypt with a mighty hand, and with an outstretched arm, and with a great revelation, and with signs and wonders" (Deut. 26:8).

וַיּוֹצִאֵנוּ יְיָ מִמִּצְרַיִם. לֹא עַל־יְדֵי מַלְאָךְ, וְלֹא עַל־יְדֵי שָׂרָף. וְלֹא עַל־יְדֵי שָׁלִיחַ. אֶלָּא הַקָּדוֹשׁ בָּרוּךְ הוּא בִּכְבוֹדוֹ וּבְעַצְמוֹ. שֶׁנֶּאֱמַר: וְעָבַרְתִּי בְאֶרֶץ מִצְרַיִם בַּלַּיְלָה הַזֶּה, וְהִכֵּיתִי כָל־בְּכוֹר בְּאֶרֶץ מִצְרַיִם, מֵאָדָם וְעַד בְּהֵמָה, וּבְכָל־אֱלֹהֵי מִצְרַיִם אֶעֱשֶׂה שְׁפָטִים אֲנִי יְיָ:

Va-yotzee-aynoo Ado-nai mee-mitzra-yim – lo al y'day ma-lach, v'lo al y'day sa-raf, v'lo al y'day shalee-ach, ela ha-kadosh baruch hoo, bich'vodo, oo-v'atzmo, she-ne-emar, V'a-vartee v'eretz mitzra-yim ba-lailah ha-zeh, v'hee-kaytee chol b'chor b'eretz mitzra-yim, may-adam v'ad b'haymah, oov'chol elo-hay mitzra-yim e-esseh sh'fatim – a-nee, Ado-nai.

"And the Lord took us out of Egypt"— not by the hand of an angel, not by the hand of a seraph, not by the hand of a messenger, but by the Holy One blessed is He, in His Glory, Himself, as it is stated, "I will pass through the land of Egypt on this night, and I will strike every firstborn in the land of Egypt, both man and beast, and upon all the gods of Egypt will I wreak judgments—I, the Lord" (Ex. 12:12).

 *"...not by the hand of an angel"*—Certain jobs just cannot be delegated. When it comes to human history, the survival of the Jewish people has and always will be one such job. Though we might sometimes despair of seeing the end of our long exile, it's important to remember Who's ultimately in charge.

וְעָבַרְתִּי בְאֶרֶץ־מִצְרַיִם בַּלַּיְלָה הַזֶּה. אֲנִי וְלֹא מַלְאָךְ. וְהִכֵּיתִי כָל בְּכוֹר בְּאֶרֶץ־מִצְרַיִם. אֲנִי וְלֹא שָׂרָף. וּבְכָל־אֱלֹהֵי מִצְרַיִם אֶעֱשֶׂה שְׁפָטִים, אֲנִי וְלֹא הַשָּׁלִיחַ. אֲנִי יְיָ. אֲנִי הוּא וְלֹא אַחֵר:

V'a-vartee v'eretz mitzra-yim ba-lailah ha-zeh – a-nee, v'lo ma-lach. V'hee-kaytee chol b'chor b'eretz mitzra-yim – a-nee, v'lo sa-raf. Oov'chol elo-hay mitzra-yim e-esseh sh'fatim – a-nee, v'lo ha-sha-liach. A-nee Ado-nai – a-nee hoo v'lo achayr.

"I will pass through the land of Egypt on this night"—I, and not an angel. "And I will strike every firstborn in the land of Egypt"—I, and not a seraph. "And upon all the gods of Egypt will I wreak judgments"—I, and not a messenger. "I, the Lord"—it is I and not another.

בְּיָד חֲזָקָה. זוֹ הַדֶּבֶר. כְּמָה שֶׁנֶּאֱמַר: הִנֵּה יַד־יְיָ הוֹיָה, בְּמִקְנְךָ אֲשֶׁר בַּשָּׂדֶה, בַּסּוּסִים בַּחֲמֹרִים בַּגְּמַלִּים, בַּבָּקָר וּבַצֹּאן, דֶּבֶר כָּבֵד מְאֹד:

B'yad chaza-kah – zo ha-dever, k'mah she-ne-emar, Heenay yad Adonai ho-yah b'mikn'cha asher ba-sadeh, ba-soo-sim, ba-cha-morim, ba-g'ma-lim, ba-bakar, oo-va-tzon, dever kavayd m'od.

"With a mighty hand"–This refers to the pestilence, as it is stated, "Behold, the hand of the Lord will be upon your live-stock that is in the field, upon the horses, the donkeys, the camels, the cattle, and the sheep, a very severe pestilence" (Ex. 9:3).

וּבִזְרֹעַ נְטוּיָה. זוֹ הַחֶרֶב. כְּמָה שֶׁנֶּאֱמַר: וְחַרְבּוֹ שְׁלוּפָה בְּיָדוֹ, נְטוּיָה עַל־יְרוּשָׁלָיִם:

Oo-viz'ro-a n'too-ya – zo ha-cherev, k'mah she-ne-emar, V'charbo sh'loofa b'yado, n'too-ya ahl y'roo-shala-yim.

"And with an outstretched arm"–This refers to the sword, as it is stated, "And a drawn sword in his hand, outstretched over Jerusalem" (I Chron. 21:16).

וּבְמֹרָא גָּדוֹל, זוֹ גִּלּוּי שְׁכִינָה. כְּמָה שֶׁנֶּאֱמַר: אוֹ הֲנִסָּה אֱלֹהִים, לָבוֹא לָקַחַת לוֹ גוֹי מִקֶּרֶב גּוֹי, בְּמַסֹּת בְּאֹתֹת וּבְמוֹפְתִים וּבְמִלְחָמָה, וּבְיָד חֲזָקָה וּבִזְרוֹעַ נְטוּיָה, וּבְמוֹרָאִים גְּדֹלִים, כְּכֹל אֲשֶׁר־עָשָׂה לָכֶם יְיָ אֱלֹהֵיכֶם בְּמִצְרַיִם, לְעֵינֶיךָ:

Oo-v'mora ga-dol – zo gee-luy sh'cheena, k'mah she-ne-emar, O haneesah Elo-him la-vo, la-kachat lo goy mee-kerev goy, b'masot, b'otot, oov'mof'tim, oov'milchamah, oov'yad chaza-kah ooviz'ro-a n'too-yah, oov'mora-im g'dolim, k'chol asher asah la-chem Ado-nai, Elo-haychem, b'mitzra-yim l'ay-necha.

"And with a great revelation"–This refers to the revelation of God's presence, as it is stated, "Or has God proven Himself to come, to take a nation from the midst of another nation, with demonstra-tions of power, with signs, wonders, and war, with a mighty hand and an out-stretched arm, and with great revelations, like all that the Lord, your God, did for you in Egypt before your eyes" (Deut. 4:34).

וּבְאֹתוֹת. זֶה הַמַּטֶּה, כְּמָה שֶׁנֶּאֱמַר: וְאֶת הַמַּטֶּה הַזֶּה תִּקַּח בְּיָדֶךָ. אֲשֶׁר תַּעֲשֶׂה־בּוֹ אֶת־הָאֹתֹת:

Oov'otot – zeh ha-mateh, k'mah she-ne-emar, V'et ha-mateh ha-zeh tee-kach b'ya-decha asher ta-asseh bo et ha-otot.

"With signs"–This refers to the staff, as it is stated, "And you shall take this staff in your hand with which you shall perform the signs" (Ex. 4:17).

וּבְמוֹפְתִים. זֶה הַדָּם. כְּמָה שֶׁנֶּאֱמַר: וְנָתַתִּי מוֹפְתִים, בַּשָּׁמַיִם וּבָאָרֶץ:

Oov'mof'tim – zeh ha-dam, k'mah she-ne-emar, V'na-ta-tee mof'tim ba-shama-yim oo-va-aretz –

"And with wonders"–This refers to the blood, as it is stated (Joel 2:30), "And I will exhibit wonders in heaven and on earth–

We spill wine from our glasses to symbolize that we do not rejoice at another's downfall–even in the case of a people who tried to destroy us. It's a lesson both of humanity and compassion. We find this lesson in the Talmud (*Megillah* 10b) when, at the conclusion of the splitting of the Red Sea, the angels wanted to sing and rejoice at the liberation of Israel. God restrained them and admonished them saying, "My creatures are drowning and you want to sing?" This example compels us to be reminded, in this moment of joy, of the pain our redemption caused. And it teaches us once again that every living creature is precious.

At the mention of each of the following three wonders—blood, fire, pillars of smoke—
we dip a finger into our wine cup and remove a drop of wine.

דָּם. וָאֵשׁ. וְתִמְרוֹת עָשָׁן:

Dam. Va-aysh. V'tim'rot a-shan.

Blood, fire and pillars of smoke." (Joel 2:30).

דָּבָר אַחֵר. בְּיָד חֲזָקָה שְׁתַּיִם. וּבִזְרֹעַ נְטוּיָה שְׁתַּיִם. וּבְמוֹרָא גָּדוֹל שְׁתַּיִם. וּבְאֹתוֹת שְׁתַּיִם. וּבְמוֹפְתִים שְׁתַּיִם: אֵלוּ עֶשֶׂר מַכּוֹת שֶׁהֵבִיא הַקָּדוֹשׁ בָּרוּךְ הוּא עַל־הַמִּצְרִים בְּמִצְרָיִם, וְאֵלוּ הֵן:

Da-var achayr: b'yad chaza-kah, sh'ta-yim; oo-viz'ro-a n'too-yah, sh'ta-yim; oov'morah ga-dol, sh'ta-yim; oov'otot, sh'ta-yim; oov'mof'tim, sh'ta-yim. Ay-loo esser ma-kot she-hayvee ha-kadosh, baruch hoo, al ha-mitzrim b'mitzra-yim. V'ay-loo hayn:

Another explanation: "with a mighty hand" refers to two plagues; "and with an outstretched arm," another two; "and with a great revelation," two; "and with signs," two; "and with wonders," two. This refers to the ten plagues that the Holy One, blessed is He, brought upon the Egyptians in Egypt. They are:

At the mention of each of the following ten plagues we dip a finger into our wine cup and remove a drop of wine. The same is done at the mention of each word in Rabbi Yehudah's mnemonic below.

דָּם. צְפַרְדֵּעַ. כִּנִּים. עָרוֹב. דֶּבֶר. שְׁחִין. בָּרָד. אַרְבֶּה. חֹשֶׁךְ. מַכַּת בְּכוֹרוֹת:

Dam. Tz'far-day-a. Keenim. Arov. Dever. Sh'chin. Ba-rad. Arbeh. Cho-shech. Makat B'chorot.

Blood. Frogs. Lice. Wild beasts. Pestilence. Boils. Hail. Locusts. Darkness. Slaying of the firstborn.

רַבִּי יְהוּדָה הָיָה נוֹתֵן בָּהֶם סִמָּנִים: דְּצַ"ךְ עַדַ"שׁ בְּאַחַ"ב:

Ra-bee Ye-hoo-da ha-yah notayn ba-hem seema-nim: d'tzach, adash b'achav.

Rabbi Judah abbreviated them, thus: D'TZACH, ADASH, B'ACHAV.

The cup is now refilled.

If the following debate seems rather odd (after all, does it really matter exactly how many plagues there were, as long as we were ultimately freed?), consider the following:

When a mother cooks dinner for her family, what kind of a "thank you" would she appreciate more? A couple of mumbled words of gratitude before everyone dashes off, or a loving listing of appreciated items, in which her husband or children demonstrate their awareness of the tremendous amount of labor that went into creating that dinner?

It pays to sometimes consider just how much God has done for us. If He has done us two hundred and fifty favors, then we are far more indebted to Him than if He had done only two hundred. The truth is, though, that the kindnesses that God showers upon us on a daily basis are too numerous for us to ever really enumerate.

רַבִּי יוֹסֵי הַגְּלִילִי אוֹמֵר: מִנַּיִן אַתָּה אוֹמֵר, שֶׁלָּקוּ הַמִּצְרִים בְּמִצְרַיִם עֶשֶׂר מַכּוֹת, וְעַל הַיָּם, לָקוּ חֲמִשִּׁים מַכּוֹת? בְּמִצְרַיִם מָה הוּא אוֹמֵר: וַיֹּאמְרוּ הַחַרְטֻמִּם אֶל־פַּרְעֹה, אֶצְבַּע אֱלֹהִים הִוא. וְעַל הַיָּם מָה הוּא אוֹמֵר? וַיַּרְא יִשְׂרָאֵל אֶת־הַיָּד הַגְּדֹלָה, אֲשֶׁר עָשָׂה יְיָ בְּמִצְרַיִם, וַיִּירְאוּ

הָעָם אֶת־יְיָ. וַיַּאֲמִינוּ בַּייָ, וּבְמשֶׁה עַבְדּוֹ. כַּמָּה לָקוּ בָּאֶצְבַּע? עֶשֶׂר מַכּוֹת: אֱמוֹר מֵעַתָּה, בְּמִצְרַיִם לָקוּ עֶשֶׂר מַכּוֹת, וְעַל־הַיָּם, לָקוּ חֲמִשִּׁים מַכּוֹת:

Ra-bee Yo-see ha-g'lee-lee omayr: Mee-na-yin atah omayr she-la-koo ha-mitzrim b'mitzra-yim esser ma-kot, v'al ha-yam la-koo cha-meeshim ma-kot? B'mitzra-yim, mah hoo omayr? Va-yom'roo ha-char-toomim el Paroh, Etzba Elo-him hee. V'al ha-yam, mah hoo omayr? Va-yar yisra-ayl et ha-yad ha-g'dolah, asher asah Ado-nai b'mitzra-yim, va-yee-r'oo ha-am et Ado-nai, va-ya-ameenoo bado-nai oov'Moshe, avdo. Ka-mah la-koo b'etzba? Esser ma-kot. Emor may-atah – b'mitzra-yim la-koo esser ma-kot, v'al ha-yam la-koo cha-meeshim ma-kot.

Rabbi Yosé the Galilean said: "From where can we deduce that the Egyptians were stricken with ten plagues in Egypt, and with fifty plagues at sea? With regard to the plagues in Egypt, what is stated? 'And the magicians said to Pharaoh, "It is the finger of God" (Ex. 8:19). With regard to the plagues at the sea, what is stated? 'And Israel saw the great hand, which the Lord had used upon the Egyptians, and the people feared God, and they believed in God and in Moses, his servant' (Ex. 14:31). How many plagues did they receive by one finger? Ten plagues. Thus it follows—in Egypt they were dealt ten plagues, and at the sea they were dealt fifty plagues."

רַבִּי אֱלִיעֶזֶר אוֹמֵר: מִנַּיִן שֶׁכָּל־מַכָּה וּמַכָּה, שֶׁהֵבִיא הַקָּדוֹשׁ בָּרוּךְ הוּא עַל הַמִּצְרִים בְּמִצְרַיִם, הָיְתָה שֶׁל אַרְבַּע מַכּוֹת? שֶׁנֶּאֱמַר: יְשַׁלַּח־בָּם חֲרוֹן אַפּוֹ, עֶבְרָה וָזַעַם וְצָרָה. מִשְׁלַחַת מַלְאֲכֵי רָעִים. עֶבְרָה אַחַת. וָזַעַם שְׁתַּיִם. וְצָרָה שָׁלשׁ. מִשְׁלַחַת מַלְאֲכֵי רָעִים אַרְבַּע: אֱמוֹר מֵעַתָּה, בְּמִצְרַיִם לָקוּ אַרְבָּעִים מַכּוֹת, וְעַל הַיָּם לָקוּ מָאתַיִם מַכּוֹת:

Ra-bee Elee-ezer omayr: Mee-na-yin shekol ma-kah oo-ma-kah she-hayvee ha-kadosh, baruch hoo, al ha-mitzrim b'mitra-yim ha-y'tah shel arba ma-kot? She-ne-emar, Y'shalach bahm char-on apo – evrah, va-za-am, v'tzarah, mishlachat mal-achay ra-im. Evrah, achat; va-za-am, sh'ta-yim;

Rabbi Eliezer said: "From where can we deduce that each plague the Holy One, blessed is He, brought upon the Egyptians in Egypt consisted of four plagues? As it is stated, 'He dispatched against them the kindling of His anger—wrath, fury, and trouble, a delegation of evil messengers.' 'Wrath' indicates one plague; 'fury,' two;

33

v'tzarah, shalosh; mishlachat mal-achay ra-im, arba. Emor may-atah – b'mitzra-yim la-koo arba-im ma-kot, v'al ha-yam la-koo ma-ta-yim ma-kot.

'trouble,' three; 'a delegation of evil messengers,' four. Thus it follows—in Egypt they were dealt forty plagues, and at sea they were dealt two hundred plagues."

רַבִּי עֲקִיבָא אוֹמֵר: מִנַּיִן שֶׁכָּל־מַכָּה וּמַכָּה, שֶׁהֵבִיא הַקָּדוֹשׁ בָּרוּךְ הוּא עַל הַמִּצְרִים בְּמִצְרַיִם, הָיְתָה שֶׁל חָמֵשׁ מַכּוֹת? שֶׁנֶּאֱמַר: יְשַׁלַּח־בָּם חֲרוֹן אַפּוֹ, עֶבְרָה וָזַעַם וְצָרָה. מִשְׁלַחַת מַלְאֲכֵי רָעִים. חֲרוֹן אַפּוֹ אַחַת. עֶבְרָה שְׁתַּיִם. וָזַעַם שָׁלֹשׁ. וְצָרָה אַרְבַּע. מִשְׁלַחַת מַלְאֲכֵי רָעִים חָמֵשׁ: אֱמוֹר מֵעַתָּה, בְּמִצְרַיִם לָקוּ חֲמִשִּׁים מַכּוֹת, וְעַל הַיָּם לָקוּ חֲמִשִּׁים וּמָאתַיִם מַכּוֹת:

Ra-bee Akeeva omayr: Mee-na-yin shekol ma-kah oo-ma-kah she-hayvee ha-kadosh, baruch hoo, al ha-mitzrim b'mitra-yim ha-y'tah shel cha-maysh ma-kot? She-ne-emar, Y'shalach bahm char-on apo – evrah, va-za-am, v'tzarah, mishlachat mal-achay ra-im. Char-on apo, achat; evrah, sh'ta-yim; va-za-am, shalosh; v'tzarah, arba; mishlachat mal-achay ra-im, cha-maysh. Emor may-atah – b'mitzra-yim la-koo cha-meeshim ma-kot, v'al ha-yam la-koo cha-meeshim oo-mata-yim ma-kot.

Rabbi Akiva said: "From where can we deduce that each plague the Holy One, blessed is He, brought upon the Egyptians in Egypt consisted of five plagues? As it is stated, 'He dispatched against them the kindling of His anger—wrath, fury, and trouble, a delegation of evil messengers.' 'The kindling of His anger' indicates one plague; 'wrath,' two; 'fury,' three; 'trouble,' four; 'a delegation of evil messengers,' five. Thus it follows—in Egypt they were dealt fifty plagues, and at sea they were dealt two hundred and fifty plagues."

The following song of "Dayenu" suggests that, with each progressive step we take, we must learn to stop and say "Enough!" We must celebrate each individual accomplishment in our lives as an enriching experience of growth. At the same time, however, we need to also realize that ultimately there is no limit to what we can achieve and no end to the pleasure we can experience with each new achievement.

כַּמָּה מַעֲלוֹת טוֹבוֹת לַמָּקוֹם עָלֵינוּ:

דַּיֵּנוּ:   אִלּוּ הוֹצִיאָנוּ מִמִּצְרַיִם, וְלֹא עָשָׂה בָהֶם שְׁפָטִים,

דַּיֵּנוּ:   אִלּוּ עָשָׂה בָהֶם שְׁפָטִים, וְלֹא עָשָׂה בֵאלֹהֵיהֶם,

דַּיֵּנוּ:   אִלּוּ עָשָׂה בֵאלֹהֵיהֶם, וְלֹא הָרַג אֶת־בְּכוֹרֵיהֶם,

דַּיֵּנוּ:   אִלּוּ הָרַג אֶת־בְּכוֹרֵיהֶם, וְלֹא נָתַן לָנוּ אֶת־מָמוֹנָם,

דַּיֵּנוּ:   אִלּוּ נָתַן לָנוּ אֶת־מָמוֹנָם, וְלֹא קָרַע לָנוּ אֶת־הַיָּם,

דַּיֵּנוּ:   אִלּוּ קָרַע לָנוּ אֶת־הַיָּם, וְלֹא הֶעֱבִירָנוּ בְתוֹכוֹ בֶּחָרָבָה,

דַּיֵּנוּ:   אִלּוּ הֶעֱבִירָנוּ בְתוֹכוֹ בֶּחָרָבָה, וְלֹא שִׁקַּע צָרֵינוּ בְּתוֹכוֹ,

אִלּוּ שִׁקַּע צָרֵינוּ בְּתוֹכוֹ, וְלֹא סִפֵּק צָרְכֵּנוּ בַּמִּדְבָּר אַרְבָּעִים שָׁנָה, דַּיֵּנוּ:

אִלּוּ סִפֵּק צָרְכֵּנוּ בַּמִּדְבָּר אַרְבָּעִים שָׁנָה, וְלֹא הֶאֱכִילָנוּ אֶת־הַמָּן, דַּיֵּנוּ:

דַּיֵּנוּ:   אִלּוּ הֶאֱכִילָנוּ אֶת־הַמָּן, וְלֹא נָתַן לָנוּ אֶת־הַשַּׁבָּת,

דַּיֵּנוּ:   אִלּוּ נָתַן לָנוּ אֶת־הַשַּׁבָּת, וְלֹא קֵרְבָנוּ לִפְנֵי הַר סִינַי,

דַּיֵּנוּ:   אִלּוּ קֵרְבָנוּ לִפְנֵי הַר סִינַי, וְלֹא נָתַן לָנוּ אֶת־הַתּוֹרָה,

דַּיֵּנוּ:   אִלּוּ נָתַן לָנוּ אֶת־הַתּוֹרָה, וְלֹא הִכְנִיסָנוּ לְאֶרֶץ יִשְׂרָאֵל,

אִלּוּ הִכְנִיסָנוּ לְאֶרֶץ יִשְׂרָאֵל, וְלֹא בָנָה לָנוּ אֶת־בֵּית הַבְּחִירָה,   דַּיֵּנוּ:

Ka-mah ma-alot tovot la-ma-kom a-laynoo!

Ee-loo hotzee-anoo mee-mitzra-yim, v'lo asah va-hem sh'fatim, da-yaynoo.

Ee-loo asah va-hem sh'fatim, v'lo asah vaylo-hayhem, da-yaynoo.

Ee-loo asah vaylo-hayhem, v'lo ha-rag et b'cho-rayhem, da-yaynoo.

Ee-loo ha-rag et b'cho-rayhem, v'lo na-tan la-noo et ma-monam, da-yaynoo.

Eeloo na-tan la-noo et ma-monam, v'lo kara la-noo et ha-yam,

How many favors has the Ever-Present bestowed upon us!

Had He brought us out of Egypt, but not executed judgment upon the Egyptians, it would have sufficed for us.

Had He executed judgment upon them, but not upon their gods, it would have sufficed for us.

Had He executed judgment upon their gods, but not slain their firstborn, it would have sufficed for us.

Had He slain their firstborn, but not given us their wealth, it would have sufficed for us.

Had He given us their wealth, but not split the sea for us, it would have sufficed

da-yaynoo.

Ee-loo kara la-noo et ha-yam, v'lo he-evee-ranoo v'tocho be-charavah, da-yaynoo.

Ee-loo he-evee-ranoo v'tocho be-charavah, v'lo shee-ka tzaraynoo b'tocho, da-yaynoo.

Ee-loo shee-ka tzaraynoo b'tocho, v'lo seepayk tzar-kaynoo ba-midbar arba-im sha-nah, da-yaynoo.

Ee-loo seepayk tzar-kaynoo ba-midbar arba-im sha-nah, v'lo he-echee-lanoo et ha-man, da-yaynoo.

Eel-oo he-echee-lanoo et ha-man, v'lo na-tan la-noo et ha-shabbat, da-yaynoo.

Ee-loo na-tan la-noo et ha-shabbat, v'lo kay-r'va-noo lif'nay har see-nai, da-yaynoo.

Ee-loo kay-r'va-noo lif'nay har see-nai, v'lo na-tan la-noo et ha-torah, da-yaynoo.

Ee-loo na-tan la-noo et ha-torah, v'lo hich-nee-sa-noo l'eretz yisra-ayl, da-yaynoo.

Ee-loo hich-nee-sanoo l'eretz yisra-ayl, v'lo va-nah la-noo et bayt ha-b'chee-rah, da-yaynoo.

for us.

Had He split the sea for us, but had not led us through it on dry land, it would have sufficed for us.

Had He led us through it on dry land, but had not drowned our oppressors in it, it would have sufficed for us.

Had He drowned our oppressors in it, but not provided for our needs in the desert for forty years, it would have been sufficient for us.

Had He provided for our needs in the desert for forty years, but had not fed us the manna, it would have sufficed for us.

Had He fed us the manna, but had not given us Shabbat, it would have sufficed for us.

Had He given us Shabbat, but had not brought us to Mount Sinai, it would have sufficed for us.

Had He brought us to Mount Sinai, but had not given us the Torah, it would have sufficed for us.

Had He given us the Torah, but had not brought us into the Land of Israel, it would have sufficed for us.

Had He brought us into the Land of Israel, but had not built the Temple for us, it would have sufficed for us.

עַל אַחַת כַּמָּה וְכַמָּה טוֹבָה כְפוּלָה וּמְכֻפֶּלֶת לַמָּקוֹם עָלֵינוּ:
שֶׁהוֹצִיאָנוּ מִמִּצְרַיִם, וְעָשָׂה בָהֶם שְׁפָטִים,
וְעָשָׂה בֵאלֹהֵיהֶם, וְהָרַג אֶת־בְּכוֹרֵיהֶם,
וְנָתַן לָנוּ אֶת־מָמוֹנָם, וְקָרַע לָנוּ אֶת־הַיָּם,
וְהֶעֱבִירָנוּ בְתוֹכוֹ בֶּחָרָבָה, וְשִׁקַע צָרֵינוּ בְּתוֹכוֹ,

וְסִפֵּק צָרְכֵּנוּ בַּמִּדְבָּר אַרְבָּעִים שָׁנָה,   וְהֶאֱכִילָנוּ אֶת־הַמָּן,
וְנָתַן לָנוּ אֶת־הַשַּׁבָּת,   וְקֵרְבָנוּ לִפְנֵי הַר סִינַי,
וְנָתַן לָנוּ אֶת־הַתּוֹרָה,   וְהִכְנִיסָנוּ לְאֶרֶץ יִשְׂרָאֵל,
וּבָנָה לָנוּ אֶת־בֵּית הַבְּחִירָה,   לְכַפֵּר עַל־כָּל־עֲוֹנוֹתֵינוּ.

Al achat ka-mah v'cha-mah tovah, chfoo-lah oo-m'choo-pelet, la-ma-kom alay-noo! She-hotzee-anoo meemitzra-yim, v'asah va-hem sh'fa-tim, v'asah vaylo-hayhem, v'ha-rag et b'cho-rayhem, v'na-tan la-noo et ma-monam, v'kara la-noo et ha-yam, v'he-evee-ranoo v'tocho be-char-avah, v'shee-ka tzaraynoo b'tocho, v'seepayk tzar-kaynoo ba-midbar arba-im sha-nah, v'he-echee-lanoo et ha-man, v'na-tan la-noo et ha-shab-bat, v'kay-r'va-noo lif'nay har see-nai, v'na-tan la-noo et ha-torah, v'hich-nee-sanoo l'eretz yisra-ayl, oova-nah la-noo et bayt ha-b'chee-rah l'cha-payr al kol avono-taynoo.

How much more so are the favors, doubled and redoubled, that the Ever-Present has bestowed upon us! He brought us out of Egypt, executed judgment upon them, executed judgment upon their gods, slew their firstborn, gave us their wealth, split the sea for us, led us through it on dry land, drowned our oppressors in it, provided for our needs in the desert for forty years, fed us the manna, gave us Shabbat, brought us to Mount Sinai, gave us the Torah, brought us into the Land of Israel, and built the Temple for us to atone for all our sins.

רַבָּן גַּמְלִיאֵל הָיָה אוֹמֵר: כָּל שֶׁלֹּא אָמַר שְׁלֹשָׁה דְבָרִים אֵלּוּ בַּפֶּסַח,
לֹא יָצָא יְדֵי חוֹבָתוֹ, וְאֵלּוּ הֵן:

Raban Gamlee-el ha-yah omayr: Kol shelo amar sh'loshah d'va-rim ay-loo ba-pesach lo yatza y'day cho-vato. V'ay-loo hayn:

Rabban Gamliel used to say: "Whoever does not discuss these three things on Passover has not fulfilled his obligation." And they are the following:

פֶּסַח. מַצָּה. וּמָרוֹר:

Pesach,
Matzah,
oo-Marror.

Pesach—The Passover sacrifice
Matzah—The unleavened bread
Marror—The bitter herbs

Passover is a traditional Biblical pilgrimage holiday and—before the Temple in Jerusalem was destroyed in 70 B.C.E.—Jews regularly made pilgrimages to Jerusalem and to the Temple to bring animal sacrifices known in Hebrew as *korbanos*. The purpose of bringing sacrifices was to bring us closer to God. In fact, the Hebrew word *korban* means to draw close. One of the most important sacrifices brought was the *Korban Pesach*, or Passover offering. The Passover sacrifice originates from the time of the Exodus. To protect themselves from the tenth plague, which killed each Egyptian eldest son, Jewish families were instructed to get a lamb and slaughter it. Then they were told to paint the doorway to their homes with its blood and to follow this with a dinner of roasted lamb and matzah. When the angel of death swept over Egypt, the homes that had blood on the posts were skipped or passed over, saving the Jewish first-born boys. However, it was not some mystical property of lambs' blood that protected the Jews, but the merit of having followed God's will.

We gaze at, but do not lift the shankbone and recite:

פֶּסַח שֶׁהָיוּ אֲבוֹתֵינוּ אוֹכְלִים, בִּזְמַן שֶׁבֵּית הַמִּקְדָּשׁ הָיָה קַיָּם, עַל שׁוּם מָה? עַל שׁוּם שֶׁפָּסַח הַקָּדוֹשׁ בָּרוּךְ הוּא, עַל בָּתֵּי אֲבוֹתֵינוּ בְּמִצְרַיִם, שֶׁנֶּאֱמַר: וַאֲמַרְתֶּם זֶבַח פֶּסַח הוּא לַיְיָ, אֲשֶׁר פָּסַח עַל בָּתֵּי בְנֵי יִשְׂרָאֵל בְּמִצְרַיִם, בְּנָגְפּוֹ אֶת־מִצְרַיִם וְאֶת־בָּתֵּינוּ הִצִּיל, וַיִּקֹּד הָעָם וַיִּשְׁתַּחֲווּ.

Pesach she-ha-yoo avotaynoo o-ch'lim biz'man she-bayt ha-mik-dash ha-yah ka-yam al shoom mah? Al shoom she-pasach ha-kadosh, baruch hoo, al ba-tay avotaynoo b'mitzra-yim, she-ne-emar: Va-amar-tem ze-vach pesach hoo ladonai, asher pasach al batay v'nay yis-ra-ayl b'mitzra-yim b'nagpo et mitzra-yim, v'et ba-taynoo hee-tzil. Va-yeekod ha-am va-yishta-chavoo.

Pesach—What is the reason for the Passover sacrifice that our forefathers ate during the time of the Temple? Because the Holy One, Blessed be He, passed over the houses of our foreforefathers in Egypt, as it is stated: "You shall say, 'It is a Passover sacrifice to the Lord, for He passed over the houses of the children of Israel in Egypt when he struck the Egyptians, and He saved our houses. And the people kneeled and prostrated themselves.'"

The great 19th century scholar, Rabbi Samson Raphael Hirsch, notes that matzah is a symbol of slavery and social dependence. The opposite of matzah is leaven, or *chametz*, which Rabbi Hirsch says is a symbol of independence.

Passover serves as a memorial, reminding us each year of how the gifts of freedom and independence were bestowed upon us by God. Thus for a cycle of eight days (seven days in Israel), we cannot partake of leaven of the bread of independence. On the holiday commemorating our personal independence and the right to our own property, we must clear out from all our homes the symbol of independence and we are forbidden to eat it. In this way, we remind ourselves, in symbolic terms, that, at the moment of our emergence to freedom and independence, we possessed neither. Only through the free commanding power of God did we become a free and independent people. We did not free ourselves; God freed us, and thus we owe Him our very existence.

The seder leader lifts up the middle matzah and recites:

מַצָּה זוּ שֶׁאָנוּ אוֹכְלִים, עַל שׁוּם מָה? עַל שׁוּם שֶׁלֹּא הִסְפִּיק בְּצֵקָם שֶׁל אֲבוֹתֵינוּ לְהַחֲמִיץ, עַד שֶׁנִּגְלָה עֲלֵיהֶם מֶלֶךְ מַלְכֵי הַמְּלָכִים, הַקָּדוֹשׁ בָּרוּךְ הוּא, וּגְאָלָם, שֶׁנֶּאֱמַר: וַיֹּאפוּ אֶת־הַבָּצֵק, אֲשֶׁר הוֹצִיאוּ מִמִּצְרַיִם, עֻגֹת מַצּוֹת, כִּי לֹא חָמֵץ: כִּי גֹרְשׁוּ מִמִּצְרַיִם, וְלֹא יָכְלוּ לְהִתְמַהְמֵהַּ, וְגַם צֵדָה לֹא עָשׂוּ לָהֶם.

Matzah zoo she-a-noo och'lim al shoom mah? Al shoom she-lo hispik b'tzaykam shel avotaynoo l'hachmitz, ad she-niglah a-layhem melech, mal'chay ha-m'lachim, ha-kadosh, baruch hoo, oo-g'alam, she-ne-emar: Va-yofoo et ha-ba-tzayk asher hotzee-oo meemitzra-yim oo-got matzot, kee lo cha-maytz, kee gorshoo meemitzra-yim v'lo yach'loo l'hitma-may-ah, v'gam tzaydah lo assoo la-hem.

Matzah—What is the reason we eat matzah? Because before our forefathers' dough had time to become leavened, the King of Kings, the Holy One, blessed is He, revealed Himself to them and redeemed them, as it is stated: "They baked the dough that they had taken out of Egypt as unleavened cakes, for it had not leavened, for they were driven out of Egypt and they could not tarry, and also they had not made provisions for themselves."

☙ Matzah symbolizes haste. We were once in a such a hurry that we couldn't prepare our food properly. When we escaped from Egypt we took matzah. It's hobo food, shepherd's food, wanderer's nutrition. Matzah reminds us of our humble background.

Rabbi Ephraim Oshry, in his book Annihilation of Lithuanian Jewry *recounts his struggle to make matzah available during World War II in the Kovno ghetto in Lithuania:*

Matzah baking was risky. The machines were noisy, and the Germans patrolled the ghetto; everything we were doing was "illegal," from the machine to the finished matzah. Even the location where we were baking was dangerous, for the Germans would wonder how the Jews came to have empty rooms for baking matzah. And where did the flour come from? And white flour at that?

Most difficult was Passover of 1944. The Akzion against the children and the old people had taken place on the third and fourth days of Nissan. Our matzah-baking plans were interrupted because everyone was so frightened. It seemed certain that not a single Jew was going to survive. So who had a mind clear enough to focus on matzah-baking? Who was sure he'd even still be alive on Passover?

Days passed. Passover drew closer. Where would we find even an olive-sized piece of matzah? Despite the troubles we were suffering, we began to bake matzah. This entailed risk to life, because Kittel, the Gestapo official, visited the camp frequently.

I recall Rav Levinson, director of the Radun Yeshiva, saying to me, "You may be wondering why I am doing this with such joy? It may be that this is the last mitzvah of my life."

The day before Passover 1944 arrived there was still not a crumb of matzah available. Late that afternoon, I was standing together with other Jews who were baking matzah, when we suddenly heard a noise outside. Kittel the murderer had stopped his Gestapo car right in front of where we were baking matzah in Block C.

Hiding was out of the question; before I could even think, the butcher was at the door. "Too bad," I thought, "if I'm going to die, let it at least be for the mitzvah of baking matzah." I began to recite Viduy, but Kittel interrupted me, "Who are you?" Before I could respond, he picked up two parcels of matzah and had walked out. I stood there dumbfounded, unable to understand what I had seen.

Then I noticed Efraim Bunim, the manager of the small workshops, being arrested. The matzah baking was not resumed, and many Jews did not have even an olive-sized piece of matzah for the seder.

This disrupted Passover was, in fact, our final Passover in the Kovno ghetto. I shall always remember how I divided the little matzah we had into olive-sized pieces that Passover so that the mitzvah of eating matzah could be fulfilled by as many people as possible.

The seder leader lifts up the bitter herbs and recites:

מָרוֹר זֶה שֶׁאָנוּ אוֹכְלִים, עַל שׁוּם מָה? עַל שׁוּם שֶׁמֵּרְרוּ הַמִּצְרִים אֶת־חַיֵּי אֲבוֹתֵינוּ בְּמִצְרַיִם, שֶׁנֶּאֱמַר: וַיְמָרְרוּ אֶת־חַיֵּיהֶם בַּעֲבֹדָה קָשָׁה, בְּחֹמֶר וּבִלְבֵנִים, וּבְכָל־עֲבֹדָה בַּשָּׂדֶה: אֵת כָּל־עֲבֹדָתָם, אֲשֶׁר עָבְדוּ בָהֶם בְּפָרֶךְ.

Maror zeh she-anoo och'lim al shoom mah? Al shoom she-mayr'roo ha-mitzrim et cha-yay avotaynoo b'mitzra-yim, she-ne-emar: Va-y'ma-r'roo et cha-yayhem ba-avodah ka-shah, b'chomer oo-vil-vaynim oov-chol avodah ba-sa-deh, ayt kol avoda-tam asher av'doo va-hem b'fa-rech.

Marror—What is the reason we eat bit-ter herbs? Because the Egyptians embit-tered our foreforefathers' lives in Egypt, as it is stated: "And they embittered their lives with hard labor, with clay and with bricks and with all kinds of labor in the fields, all their work that they worked with them with back-breaking labor."

The bitter herbs are not a call to ascetic denial, but rather a reminder of life's earliest learned truths, that we must master our desires for the delicious—not deny them, but control them. For a cow, a life guided by moment-to-moment physical needs and urges is fine, but we can reach a little higher.

בְּכָל־דּוֹר וָדוֹר חַיָּב אָדָם לִרְאוֹת אֶת־עַצְמוֹ, כְּאִלּוּ הוּא יָצָא מִמִּצְרַיִם, שֶׁנֶּאֱמַר: וְהִגַּדְתָּ לְבִנְךָ בַּיּוֹם הַהוּא לֵאמֹר: בַּעֲבוּר זֶה עָשָׂה יְיָ לִי, בְּצֵאתִי מִמִּצְרַיִם. לֹא אֶת־אֲבוֹתֵינוּ בִּלְבָד, גָּאַל הַקָּדוֹשׁ בָּרוּךְ הוּא, אֶלָּא אַף אוֹתָנוּ גָּאַל עִמָּהֶם, שֶׁנֶּאֱמַר: וְאוֹתָנוּ הוֹצִיא מִשָּׁם, לְמַעַן הָבִיא אֹתָנוּ, לָתֶת לָנוּ אֶת־הָאָרֶץ אֲשֶׁר נִשְׁבַּע לַאֲבוֹתֵינוּ.

B'chol dor va-dor, cha-yav adam leer-ot et atzmo k'ee-loo hoo yatza meemitzra-yim, she-ne-emar: V'hee-gad-ta l'vin-cha ba-yom ha-hoo, lay-mor, Ba-avoor zeh, asah Ado-nai lee b'tzaytee meemitzra-yim. Lo et avo-taynoo bil-vad ga-al ha-kadosh,

In every generation, it is one's duty to regard oneself as if he himself had come out of Egypt, as it is stated: "And you shall tell your son on that day, saying, 'Because of this, the Lord did this for me when I went out of Egypt.'" Not only our foreforefathers did the Holy One, blessed

baruch hoo, ela af ota-noo ga-al ee-ma-hem, she-ne-emar: V'ota-noo hotzee mee-sham l'ma-an ha-vee ota-noo, la-tet la-noo et ha-aretz asher nishba la-avotaynoo.

is He, redeem, but He redeemed us, too, along with them, as it is stated: "And He brought us out of there so that He might bring us, to give us the land that He promised to our foreforefathers."

We cover the matzot, lift our cup of wine, and recite:

לְפִיכָךְ אֲנַחְנוּ חַיָּבִים לְהוֹדוֹת, לְהַלֵּל, לְשַׁבֵּחַ, לְפָאֵר, לְרוֹמֵם, לְהַדֵּר, לְבָרֵךְ, לְעַלֵּה וּלְקַלֵּס, לְמִי שֶׁעָשָׂה לַאֲבוֹתֵינוּ וְלָנוּ אֶת־כָּל־הַנִּסִּים הָאֵלּוּ. הוֹצִיאָנוּ מֵעַבְדוּת לְחֵרוּת, מִיָּגוֹן לְשִׂמְחָה, וּמֵאֵבֶל לְיוֹם טוֹב, וּמֵאֲפֵלָה לְאוֹר גָּדוֹל, וּמִשִּׁעְבּוּד לִגְאֻלָּה. וְנֹאמַר לְפָנָיו שִׁירָה חֲדָשָׁה. הַלְלוּיָהּ:

L'fee-chach anach-noo cha-yavim l'hodot, l'ha-layl, l'sha-bay-ach, l'fa-ayr, l'ro-maym, l'ha-dayr, l'va-raych, l'a-lay, ool-ka-layss l'mee she-asah la-avotaynoo v'la-noo et kol ha-nee-sim ha-ay-loo. Hotzee-a-noo may-avdoot l'chay-root, mee-ya-gon l'simchah, oo-may-ayvel l'yom tov, oo-may-afaylah l'or ga-dol, oo-meeshee-bood lig-oo-lah. V'nomar l'fa-nav shee-rah chada-sha. Ha-l'loo-yah.

Therefore it is our duty to thank, praise, laud, glorify, exalt, honor, bless, extol, and adore Him Who performed all these miracles for our foreforefathers and for us. He brought us out from slavery to freedom, from anguish to joy, from mourning to celebration, from darkness to great light, from bondage to redemption. Let us therefore, sing before Him a new song. Hallelujah!

הַלְלוּיָהּ. הַלְלוּ עַבְדֵי יְיָ. הַלְלוּ אֶת־שֵׁם יְיָ. יְהִי שֵׁם יְיָ מְבֹרָךְ מֵעַתָּה וְעַד עוֹלָם: מִמִּזְרַח שֶׁמֶשׁ עַד מְבוֹאוֹ. מְהֻלָּל שֵׁם יְיָ. רָם עַל־כָּל־גּוֹיִם יְיָ. עַל הַשָּׁמַיִם כְּבוֹדוֹ: מִי כַּיְיָ אֱלֹהֵינוּ. הַמַּגְבִּיהִי לָשָׁבֶת: הַמַּשְׁפִּילִי לִרְאוֹת בַּשָּׁמַיִם וּבָאָרֶץ: מְקִימִי מֵעָפָר דָּל. מֵאַשְׁפֹּת יָרִים אֶבְיוֹן: לְהוֹשִׁיבִי עִם־נְדִיבִים. עִם נְדִיבֵי עַמּוֹ: מוֹשִׁיבִי עֲקֶרֶת הַבַּיִת אֵם הַבָּנִים שְׂמֵחָה. הַלְלוּיָהּ:

Ha-l'loo-yah! Ha-l'loo, av'day Ado-nai, ha-l'loo et shaym Ado-nai. Y'-hee shaym Ado-nai m'vorach

Hallelujah! Praise, you servants of the Lord, praise the name of the Lord. May the name of the Lord be blessed from now

42

may-atah v'ad olam. Mee-mizrach shemesh ad m'vo-o, m'hoo-lal shaym Ado-nai. Rahm al kol go-yim Ado-nai; al ha-shama-yim k'vodo. Mee kado-nai, Elo-haynoo, ha-mag-beehee la-sha-vet? Ha-mash-peelee leer-ot ba-shama-yim oova-aretz? M'kee-mee may-afar dal, may-ash-pot ya-rim evyon; l'ho-sheevee im n'deevim, im n'deevay amo. Mo-sheevee ake-ret ha-ba-yit aym ha-ba-nim s'maycha. Ha-l'loo-yah!

to eternity. From the rising of the sun until its setting, the name of the Lord is praised. The Lord is high above all nations; His glory is above the heavens. Who is like the Lord, our God, Who dwells on high? Who lowers His eyes to look upon the heavens and the earth? He lifts the pau-per from the dust, from the dung heap He raises the needy; to seat him with princes, with the princes of His people. He seats the barren woman of the house as a happy mother of children. Hallelujah!

בְּצֵאת יִשְׂרָאֵל מִמִּצְרָיִם, בֵּית יַעֲקֹב מֵעַם לֹעֵז: הָיְתָה יְהוּדָה לְקָדְשׁוֹ. יִשְׂרָאֵל מַמְשְׁלוֹתָיו: הַיָּם רָאָה וַיָּנֹס, הַיַּרְדֵּן יִסֹּב לְאָחוֹר: הֶהָרִים רָקְדוּ כְאֵילִים. גְּבָעוֹת כִּבְנֵי־צֹאן: מַה־לְּךָ הַיָּם כִּי תָנוּס. הַיַּרְדֵּן תִּסֹּב לְאָחוֹר: הֶהָרִים תִּרְקְדוּ כְאֵילִים. גְּבָעוֹת כִּבְנֵי־צֹאן: מִלִּפְנֵי אָדוֹן חוּלִי אָרֶץ. מִלִּפְנֵי אֱלוֹהַּ יַעֲקֹב: הַהֹפְכִי הַצּוּר אֲגַם־מָיִם. חַלָּמִישׁ לְמַעְיְנוֹ־מָיִם.

B'tzayt yisra-ayl mee-mitzra-yim, bayt Ya-akov may-am lo-ayz, ha-y'ta y'hoo-dah l'kadsho, yisra-ayl mamsh'lotav. Ha-yam ra-ah va-ya-nos; ha-yar-dayn yee-sov l'achor. He-ha-rim rak'doo ch'aylim, g'va-ot kiv-nay tzon. Mah l'cha, ha-yam, kee ta-noos? Ha-yar-dayn, tee-sov l'achor? He-ha-rim, tir-k'doo ch'aylim; g'va-ot, kiv-nay tzon? Mee-lifnay adon, choolee aretz, mee-lifnay Elo-ah Ya-akov, ha-hof'chee ha-tzoor agam ma-yim, cha-la-mish l'mai-no ma-yim.

When Israel left Egypt, the house of Jacob left a strange-tongued people, Judah became His holy nation, Israel His dominion. The sea saw and fled; the Jordan turned back-wards. The mountains danced like rams, hills like young sheep. What frightens you, O sea, that you flee? O Jordan, that you turn backwards? You mountains, that you dance like rams; you hills, like young sheep? From before the Master, Who cre-ated the earth, from before Jacob's God, Who transforms the rock into a pond of water, the flint into a fountain of water.

The matzos are covered during the recitation of this blessing.
(On Saturday night the phrase in parentheses substitutes the preceding phrase.)

בָּרוּךְ אַתָּה יְיָ, אֱלֹהֵינוּ מֶלֶךְ הָעוֹלָם, אֲשֶׁר גְּאָלָנוּ וְגָאַל אֶת־אֲבוֹתֵינוּ

מִמִּצְרַיִם, וְהִגִּיעָנוּ הַלַּיְלָה הַזֶּה, לֶאֱכָל־בּוֹ מַצָּה וּמָרוֹר. כֵּן, יְיָ אֱלֹהֵינוּ וֵאלֹהֵי אֲבוֹתֵינוּ, יַגִּיעֵנוּ לְמוֹעֲדִים וְלִרְגָלִים אֲחֵרִים, הַבָּאִים לִקְרָאתֵנוּ לְשָׁלוֹם. שְׂמֵחִים בְּבִנְיַן עִירֶךָ, וְשָׂשִׂים בַּעֲבוֹדָתֶךָ, וְנֹאכַל שָׁם מִן הַזְּבָחִים וּמִן הַפְּסָחִים (מִן הַפְּסָחִים וּמִן הַזְּבָחִים), אֲשֶׁר יַגִּיעַ דָּמָם, עַל קִיר מִזְבַּחֲךָ לְרָצוֹן, וְנוֹדֶה לְךָ שִׁיר חָדָשׁ עַל גְּאֻלָּתֵנוּ, וְעַל פְּדוּת נַפְשֵׁנוּ: בָּרוּךְ אַתָּה יְיָ, גָּאַל יִשְׂרָאֵל:

Baruch atah, Ado-nai Elo-haynoo, melech ha-olam, asher g'a-la-noo v'ga-al et avotaynoo meemitzra-yim, v'heegee-a-noo ha-lailah ha-zeh le-echol bo matzah oo-maror. Kayn, Ado-nai, Elo-haynoo vay-lo-hay avotaynoo, yagee-aynoo l'mo-adim v'lir-ga-lim achayrim ha-ba-im li-k'ra-taynoo l'shalom, s'maychim b'vinyan ee-recha v'sasim ba-avoda-techa. V'nochal sham min ha-z'vachim oo-min ha-p'sachim (min ha-p'sachim oo-min ha-z'vachim) asher ya-gee-a da-mam al keer mizba-chacha l'ratzon. V'nodeh l'cha sheer chadash al g'oo-la-taynoo v'al p'doot naf-shaynoo. Baruch atah, Ado-nai, ga-al yisra-ayl.

Blessed are You, Lord our God, King of the universe, Who redeemed us and redeemed our forefathers from Egypt, and enabled us to reach this night that we may eat matzah and bitter herbs. Likewise, Lord, our God and the God of our forefathers, enable us to celebrate festivals and holidays in peace, joyous in the building of Your city and happy in Your service. There we will partake of the sacrifices and from the Passover sacrifices (of the Passover sacrifices and from the sacrtifices) whose blood will be sprinkled upon the side of Your altar for Your acceptance. There we will sing a new song to You for our redemption and for the deliverance of our souls. Blessed are You, Lord, Who redeemed Israel.

בָּרוּךְ אַתָּה יְיָ, אֱלֹהֵינוּ מֶלֶךְ הָעוֹלָם, בּוֹרֵא פְּרִי הַגָּפֶן:

Baruch atah, Ado-nai Elo-haynoo, melech ha-olam, bo-ray p'ree haga-fen.

Blessed are You, Lord our God, King of the universe, Who created the fruit of the vine.

While reclining on our left side, we drink the second cup of wine.

44

❧ רחצה ❧

Rachtzah
Wash hands before eating matzah

We wash our hands before eating matzah. In many homes, a basin and cup of water is passed around the table. The water is then poured over our right hand twice; we repeat the same process with the left hand. We then dry our hands with a towel.

We wash our hands and recite the customary blessing:

בָּרוּךְ אַתָּה יְיָ אֱלֹהֵינוּ מֶלֶךְ הָעוֹלָם, אֲשֶׁר קִדְּשָׁנוּ בְּמִצְוֹתָיו, וְצִוָּנוּ עַל נְטִילַת יָדָיִם:

Baruch atah, Ado-nai Elo-haynoo, melech ha-olam, asher kid'sha-noo b'mitzvotav, v'tzeeva-noo al n'teelat ya-da-yim.

Blessed are You, Lord our God, King of the universe, Who has sanctified us with His commandments, and commanded us concerning the washing of hands.

⋑ מוֹצִיא ⋑

Motzi
Recite the blessing Hamotzi

The seder leader now recites the blessing "Hamotzi" over the matzot.

The seder leader takes the two whole matzot and the broken middle matzah, lifts them and recites:

בָּרוּךְ אַתָּה יְיָ, אֱלֹהֵינוּ מֶלֶךְ הָעוֹלָם, הַמּוֹצִיא לֶחֶם מִן הָאָרֶץ:

Baruch atah, Ado-nai Elo-haynoo, melech ha-olam, ha-motzee lechem min ha-aretz.

Blessed are You, Lord our God, King of the universe, Who brought forth bread from the earth.

The Jewish People are divided into three subgroups: *Kohein*, describing the spiritual leaders who were responsible for the daily activities in the Temple; *Levi*, who assisted the *Kohein* and bore a particular responsibility for the teaching of Torah to the people; and *Israel*, who constitute the majority of the Jewish nation. Today, every Jew is descended from one of these three groups.

The fact that there are three matzot on the seder night symbolizes many things, but one of the symbolism is that each piece of matzah represents one of these groups, with the underlying message being one of diversity in unity. It's important to appreciate that the division of the Jewish People into categories of Kohein, Levi and Israel never represented the existence of a caste system. Different always just meant different, not better. Each group has a specific role to play in serving God. Nevertheless, though we may have various talents, functions, and areas of specialization, we must ultimately be united around the banner of achieving the common goals of the Jewish People.

๛ מַצָּה ๛

Matzah

Recite the blessing and eat the matzah

The seder leader recites the blessing "Al achilat matzah."

The seder leader puts down the lowest matzah and recites the following blessing
(keeping in mind the matzah of the sandwich and the Afikomen when reciting the blessing):

בָּרוּךְ אַתָּה יְיָ, אֱלֹהֵינוּ מֶלֶךְ הָעוֹלָם, אֲשֶׁר קִדְּשָׁנוּ בְּמִצְוֹתָיו וְצִוָּנוּ עַל
אֲכִילַת מַצָּה:

Baruch atah, Ado-nai Elo-haynoo, melech ha-olam, asher kid'sha-noo b'mitzvotav, v'tzeeva-noo al achee-lat matzah.

Blessed are You, Lord our God, King of the universe, Who has sanctified us with His commandments, and commanded us concerning the eating of matzah.

The seder leader then distributes at least an olive-sized portion (preferably two olive-sized portions) of the matzah to each of the assembled, and, while reclining on our left side, we eat the matzah.

Matzah is the soul. When pared of external trappings and physical interests, something yet remains of the human being. The longing of the soul. The basic nucleus of self. Likewise a loaf of bread—when denied all of its additives, of sugar and salt, and even the time to rise, an essence still remains. Stripped-down bread is matzah, and the essence of a stripped-down human being is the soul.

For an entire week, we eat only matzah and consider only our deepest aspirations and loftiest dreams. Passover offers us a golden opportunity to get back to the basics, to focus not only on priorities but on the basic values and goals which define our priorities. Ultimately, we hope to reconnect with the pure inner force that can animate our every move and actualize the boundless potential for good within us.

מרור

Marror
Eat the bitter herbs

We now eat the bitter herbs dipped in charoset. Eating charoset reminds us that "the Egyptians made slaves of the children of Israel with crushing hardness. They embittered their lives by means of hard labor with clay and with bricks and with all manners of labor in the field" (Exodus 1:13-14). The mixture of charoset contains apples, nuts and wine and symbolizes the mortar from which bricks were made.

We dip bitter herbs in charoset and recite the following blessing.
The marror should be eaten without reclining since it represents the bitterness of slavery.

בָּרוּךְ אַתָּה יְיָ אֱלֹהֵינוּ מֶלֶךְ הָעוֹלָם, אֲשֶׁר קִדְּשָׁנוּ בְּמִצְוֹתָיו וְצִוָּנוּ עַל אֲכִילַת מָרוֹר:

Baruch atah, Ado-nai Elo-haynoo, melech ha-olam, asher kid'sha-noo b'mitzvotav, v'tzeeva-noo al achee-lat maror.

Blessed are You, Lord our God, King of the universe, Who has sanctified us with His commandments, and commanded us concerning the eating of bitter herbs.

⋙ כּוֹרֵךְ ⋘

Korech

Eat the matzah and marror sandwich

Having eaten the matzah and marror separately, we now combine the two in a sandwich, in order to fulfill the commandment as the great sage Hillel understood it. It was his opinion that the Torah wants us to eat the meat from the Passover offering, the matzah, and the marror simultaneously. These days, lacking the Passover offering, we still fulfill as much of Hillel's custom as we possibly can. On this most important of nights, we try to do whatever we can to properly fulfill our obligations.

*We dip the marror in charoset, place it between two pieces of matzot
and as we hold it we make the following declaration:*

זֵכֶר לְמִקְדָּשׁ כְּהִלֵּל: כֵּן עָשָׂה הִלֵּל בִּזְמַן שֶׁבֵּית הַמִּקְדָּשׁ הָיָה קַיָּם.
הָיָה כּוֹרֵךְ פֶּסַח מַצָּה וּמָרוֹר וְאוֹכֵל בְּיַחַד. לְקַיֵּם מַה שֶׁנֶּאֱמַר:
עַל־מַצּוֹת וּמְרוֹרִים יֹאכְלֻהוּ:

Zaycher l'mikdash, k'Hillayl. Kayn asah Hillayl biz'man she-bayt ha-mikdash ha-yah ka-yam. Ha-yah ko-raych pesach matzah oo-maror v'ochayl b'yachad, l'ka-yaym mah she-ne-emar: Al matzot oo-m'rorim yoch'loohoo.

In remembrance of the Temple, according to the custom of Hillel. This is what Hillel did at the time the Temple still stood. He would combine Pesach with matzah and marror and eat them together, in order to fulfill that which is stated: "They shall eat it with matzah and marror."

While reclining on our left side, we eat the matzah and marror sandwich.

If matzah represents spirituality and marror connotes physicality, then Korech really presents us with the perfect symbolism for a human being–the physical and the spiritual bound up together, the essential duality that the Torah tells us defines the human condition. Our challenge is to master this duality, to achieve a spiritually driven balance, to live like a soul while dressed in a body.

שלחן עורך
Shulchan Orech
Eat the holiday meal

For Jews of Ashkenazi origin, (generally of German, French or East European descent) the Passover meal commences with a serving of boiled potatoes or hard-boiled eggs dipped in salt water. The salt water reminds us of the bitter tears of our slavery. Other courses vary by family custom, country of origin, and personal tastes. Some Jews of Eastern European descent, for instance, eat no fish during Passover, since it was usually soaked in alcohol. Instead, they serve ground chicken balls instead of the usual gefilte fish. Many Greek or Northern African Jews cook a whole lamb, or mix inner lamb organs into other dishes (soups, casseroles) because lamb is reminiscent of the Passover offering (called in Hebrew, *korban*) eaten during the time of the Temple. Interestingly enough, certain Jews specifically won't eat roasted foods during the seder, because they want nothing that resembles the Passover offering. They believe that until the great Holy Temple is rebuilt nothing resembling the offerings should be used in any ceremonial way.

After the potatoes or eggs, the typical appetizer at an Ashkenazi seder meal is fish, followed by soup and a chicken or meat course. Certain Jews, especially among the Chassidim, prefer not to mix matzah or matzah products with any liquid. They call these "mixed foods" *gebroks* (in Yiddish) and such foods are eaten only on the last day of Passover. So at their homes, you'll find no matzoh balls or kneidelach in your soup, no matzoh kugels and the like.

In addition, after the Temple was destroyed, Rabbinic authorities prohibited the eating of grains, such as legumes, beans, pea, as well as lesser-grains, such as rice, millet, corn and buckwheat. These grains, called *kitniyot*, are prohibited because of their similarity to wheat. Sephardim, however, never adopted this Ashkenazic stringency.

Many fascinating customs have appeared over the years. Certain Middle-Eastern Jews won't eat chickpeas simply because its name, "humus" sounds like "hametz"! Years ago, when Jews did not have a large kosher food manufacturing infrastructure they simply did not buy processed foods. Even today, following this old habit, some traditional Jews do not use processed foods, such as oil, to cook with on Passover, and instead utilize chicken fat. The variety of customs of Jews from around the world are endless, with each adding resonance and historical perspective to the traditional laws of Passover.

We now eat the seder meal, keeping in mind that the Afikomen must be eaten before midnight.
The seder plate is removed from the table.

‎צפון‎
Tzafun
Eat the Afikomen

The Afikomen represents the Passover lamb, which was eaten by every Jew when the Temple stood in Jerusalem. Jewish law stated that it was to be eaten only after the Passover meal has been concluded, and that nothing could be eaten after it. In effect, it was the traditional Passover "dessert." Today, the same rules apply to the matzah we eat for the Afikomen. We eat it only after concluding out entire meal, and it is to be the last food we taste at the seder. The Afikomen is not consumed because we are hungry, but because it is a mitzvah, a spiritual directive.

Now we eat the portion of the broken matzah called the Afikomen
that had been set aside at the beginning of the seder, during Yachatz.

Generally, we eat to satisfy our appetite—but not tonight. Tonight the Afikomen points to eating not as an end but as an enabler; it points to physical pleasures as an aid, not as an aim. Ultimately, the impression we should have of the physical world is that of a vast toolshed overflowing with devices designed to access a higher reality. The hidden potential of our physicality is to connect us to a spiritual dimension that exists in every corner of creation.

In fact, everything in this world has the potential to be used in a positive or negative way. Fire can burn, but it can also keep us warm. Food can be seen as an end in itself, or as a means of lending us the strength we need to live a spiritual life.

Therein lies the secret of eating the Afikomen—the hidden piece of matzah. Every aspect of life, every person and every fruit, every moment and every blade of grass, possesses ultimate potential. Like the latent forces of energy stored up in every atom, there is the potential of spirituality waiting inside every morsel of life, and once we experience this, once we taste the subtle flavors of the Afikomen, we won't want to taste anything else.

⊰ ברך ⊱

Barech

Recite Grace after Meals

Having eaten the Afikomen, we now recite Birkat Hamazon, the Grace after Meals. The source for reciting these blessings is the verse, "You shall eat and be satisfied, and bless God your Lord." After the satisfaction of a wonderful Passover meal, it is only right that we thank the ultimate Source of all bounty and prosperity, and recognize that it is not through "my strength and the power of my hands" that we have food to eat, but only through God's unending kindness.

The third cup of wine is now poured and Grace after Meals is recited.

שִׁיר הַמַּעֲלוֹת בְּשׁוּב יְיָ אֶת שִׁיבַת צִיּוֹן הָיִינוּ כְּחֹלְמִים: אָז יִמָּלֵא
שְׂחוֹק פִּינוּ וּלְשׁוֹנֵנוּ רִנָּה אָז יֹאמְרוּ בַגּוֹיִם הִגְדִּיל יְיָ לַעֲשׂוֹת עִם אֵלֶּה:
הִגְדִּיל יְיָ לַעֲשׂוֹת עִמָּנוּ הָיִינוּ שְׂמֵחִים: שׁוּבָה יְיָ אֶת שְׁבִיתֵנוּ כַּאֲפִיקִים
בַּנֶּגֶב: הַזֹּרְעִים בְּדִמְעָה בְּרִנָּה יִקְצֹרוּ: הָלוֹךְ יֵלֵךְ וּבָכֹה נֹשֵׂא מֶשֶׁךְ
הַזָּרַע בֹּא יָבֹא בְרִנָּה נֹשֵׂא אֲלֻמֹּתָיו:

Sheer ha-ma-alot. B'shoov Adonai et sheevat tzee-on, ha-yeenoo k'chol'mim. Az yi-ma-lay s'chok peenoo ool-sho-naynoo reenah. Az yom'roo va-go-yim, higdeel Ado-nai la-asot im ay-leh. Higdeel Ado-nai la-asot eema-noo; ha-yeenoo s'maychim. Shoova, Ado-nai, et sh'vee-taynoo ka-afeekim ba-negev. Ha-zor'im b'dimah b'reenah yik-tzoroo. Ha-loch yaylech oovacho, nosay meshech ha-zara, bo yavo v'reenah nosay aloomotav.

A song of ascents. When the Lord brings back the returnees to Zion, we shall be like dreamers. Then our mouths will be filled with laughter and our tongues with songs of praise. Then they will say among the nations, "The Lord has done great things with these." The Lord has indeed done great things with us; we have been gladdened. Return us, O Lord, from our captivity like streams in the desert. Those who sow with tears will reap with song. He who goes along weeping, carrying valuable seeds, will return with song carrying his sheaves.

If three or more males are present, the following introductory phrases are added.
When ten or more males are present, the words in parentheses are inserted as well.

הַמְזַמֵן: רַבּוֹתַי נְבָרֵךְ!

הַמְסוּבִין: יְהִי שֵׁם יְיָ מְבֹרָךְ מֵעַתָּה וְעַד עוֹלָם.

הַמְזַמֵן: יְהִי שֵׁם יְיָ מְבֹרָךְ מֵעַתָּה וְעַד עוֹלָם. בִּרְשׁוּת מָרָנָן וְרַבָּנָן וְרַבּוֹתַי, נְבָרֵךְ (אֱלֹהֵינוּ) שֶׁאָכַלְנוּ מִשֶּׁלוֹ.

הַמְסוּבִין: בָּרוּךְ (אֱלֹהֵינוּ) שֶׁאָכַלְנוּ מִשֶּׁלוֹ וּבְטוּבוֹ חָיִינוּ.

הַמְזַמֵן: בָּרוּךְ (אֱלֹהֵינוּ) שֶׁאָכַלְנוּ מִשֶּׁלוֹ וּבְטוּבוֹ חָיִינוּ.

Leader: Rabotai, n'va-raych.

Others: Y'hee shaym Ado-nai m'vorach may-atah v'ad olam.

Leader: Y'hee shaym Ado-nai m'vorach may-atah v'ad olam. Beer-shoot ma-ranan v'ra-banan v'rabo-tai, n'va-raych (Elo-haynoo) she-achalnoo mee-shelo.

Others: Baruch (Elo-haynoo) she-achalnoo mee-shelo oov-toovo cha-yeenoo.

Leader: Baruch (Elo-haynoo) she-achalnoo mee-shelo oov-toovo cha-yeenoo.

The leader begins: Gentlemen, let us say grace.

The others reply: May the name of the Lord be blessed from now until eternity.

The leader proceeds: May the name of the Lord be blessed from now until eternity. With your permission, let us bless God of Whose bounty we have partaken.

The others reply: Blessed is our God of Whose bounty we have partaken and through whose goodness we live.

The leader repeats: Blessed is our God of Whose bounty we have partaken and through Whose goodness we live.

בָּרוּךְ אַתָּה יְיָ, אֱלֹהֵינוּ מֶלֶךְ הָעוֹלָם, הַזָּן אֶת הָעוֹלָם כֻּלוֹ בְּטוּבוֹ בְּחֵן בְּחֶסֶד וּבְרַחֲמִים הוּא נוֹתֵן לֶחֶם לְכָל בָּשָׂר כִּי לְעוֹלָם חַסְדוֹ. וּבְטוּבוֹ הַגָּדוֹל תָּמִיד לֹא חָסַר לָנוּ, וְאַל יֶחְסַר לָנוּ מָזוֹן לְעוֹלָם וָעֶד. בַּעֲבוּר שְׁמוֹ הַגָּדוֹל, כִּי הוּא אֵל זָן וּמְפַרְנֵס לַכֹּל וּמֵטִיב לַכֹּל, וּמֵכִין מָזוֹן לְכָל בְּרִיּוֹתָיו אֲשֶׁר בָּרָא. בָּרוּךְ אַתָּה יְיָ, הַזָּן אֶת הַכֹּל:

Baruch atah, Ado-nai, Elo-haynoo, melech ha-olam, ha-zan et ha-olam koolo b'toovo, b'chayn, b'che-sed, oov-rachamim. Hoo notayn lechem

Blessed are You, Lord, our God, King of the universe, Who sustains the entire world with His goodness, with grace, with kindness, and with mercy. He provides

The Hebrew word for blessing, bracha, is closely related to the word breicha, *which is a free-flowing spring of water. That is the sense of feeling blessed —a sense of free-flowing, overwhelming potential and vibrant optimism, firmly rooted in reality while reaching for the stars.*

l'chol basar, kee l'olam chasdo. Oov-toovo ha-gadol, tamid lo chasar la-noo, v'al yech-sar la-noo ma-zon l'olam va-ed, ba-avoor sh'mo ha-gadol. Kee hoo Ayl zan oom-far-nayss la-kol, oomaytiv la-kol, oomaychin ma-zon l'chol b'ree-otav asher bara. Baruch atah, Ado-nai, ha-zan et ha-kol.

food for all flesh, for His kindness is eternal. And through His abundant goodness, we have never lacked, and we will never lack food forever and ever, for the sake of His great Name. For He is God Who nourishes and supports all, and does good for all, and prepares food for all His creatures whom He has created. Blessed are You, God, Who sustains all.

נוֹדֶה לְּךָ יְיָ אֱלֹהֵינוּ עַל שֶׁהִנְחַלְתָּ לַאֲבוֹתֵינוּ, אֶרֶץ חֶמְדָּה טוֹבָה וּרְחָבָה, וְעַל שֶׁהוֹצֵאתָנוּ יְיָ אֱלֹהֵינוּ מֵאֶרֶץ מִצְרַיִם, וּפְדִיתָנוּ, מִבֵּית עֲבָדִים, וְעַל בְּרִיתְךָ שֶׁחָתַמְתָּ בִּבְשָׂרֵנוּ, וְעַל תּוֹרָתְךָ שֶׁלִּמַּדְתָּנוּ, וְעַל חֻקֶּיךָ שֶׁהוֹדַעְתָּנוּ וְעַל חַיִּים חֵן וָחֶסֶד שֶׁחוֹנַנְתָּנוּ, וְעַל אֲכִילַת מָזוֹן שָׁאַתָּה זָן וּמְפַרְנֵס אוֹתָנוּ תָּמִיד, בְּכָל יוֹם וּבְכָל עֵת וּבְכָל שָׁעָה:

Nodeh l'cha, Ado-nai, Elo-haynoo, al she-hin-chalta la-avotaynoo eretz chemdah, tovah, oor-chavah. V'al she-hotzay-tanoo, Ado-nai, Elo-haynoo, may-eretz mitzra-yim, oof-dee-tanoo meebayt avadim, v'al b'reet'cha shecha-tamta biv-saraynoo, v'al torat'cha she-leemad-tanoo, v'al choo-kecha she-hoda-tanoo, v'al cha-yim, chayn, va-chesed shecho-nan-tanoo, v'al acheelat mazon she-atah zan oom-far-nayss otanoo tamid b'chol yom, oov-chol ayt, oov-chol sha-ah.

We thank You, Lord, our God, for bequeathing to our fathers a desirable, good, and spacious land; and for taking us, Lord, our God, out of the land of Egypt, and redeeming us from the house of bondage, and for Your covenant that You sealed in our flesh, and for Your Torah that You taught us, and for Your statutes which You made known to us, and for the life, grace, and kindness which You bestowed upon us, and for the partaking of the food with which You feed and support us continually, every day, at all times, and at every hour.

וְעַל הַכֹּל יְיָ אֱלֹהֵינוּ אֲנַחְנוּ מוֹדִים לָךְ, וּמְבָרְכִים אוֹתָךְ, יִתְבָּרַךְ שִׁמְךָ בְּפִי כָל חַי תָּמִיד לְעוֹלָם וָעֶד. כַּכָּתוּב, וְאָכַלְתָּ וְשָׂבָעְתָּ, וּבֵרַכְתָּ אֶת יְיָ אֱלֹהֶיךָ עַל הָאָרֶץ הַטֹּבָה אֲשֶׁר נָתַן לָךְ. בָּרוּךְ אַתָּה יְיָ, עַל הָאָרֶץ וְעַל הַמָּזוֹן:

V'al ha-kol, Ado-nai, Elo-haynoo, anach-noo modim lach oom-var'chim otach. Yitbarach shim-cha b'fee kol chai, tamid, l'olam va-ed. Ka-katoov, V'achalta v'sa-vata, oovay-rach-ta et Ado-nai, Elo-hecha, al ha-aretz ha-tovah asher natan lach. Baruch atah, Ado-nai, al ha-aretz v'al ha-mazon.

For everything, Lord, our God, we thank You and bless You. Blessed be Your Name in the mouth of all the living, continuously, forever and ever. As it is written, "And you will eat and be satisfied, and you shall bless the Lord, your God, for the good land that He has given you." Blessed are You, Lord, for the land and for the food.

רַחֵם נָא יְיָ אֱלֹהֵינוּ, עַל יִשְׂרָאֵל עַמֶּךָ, וְעַל יְרוּשָׁלַיִם עִירֶךָ, וְעַל צִיּוֹן מִשְׁכַּן כְּבוֹדֶךָ, וְעַל מַלְכוּת בֵּית דָּוִד מְשִׁיחֶךָ, וְעַל הַבַּיִת הַגָּדוֹל וְהַקָּדוֹשׁ שֶׁנִּקְרָא שִׁמְךָ עָלָיו. אֱלֹהֵינוּ, אָבִינוּ, רְעֵנוּ, זוּנֵנוּ, פַּרְנְסֵנוּ, וְכַלְכְּלֵנוּ, וְהַרְוִיחֵנוּ, וְהַרְוַח לָנוּ יְיָ אֱלֹהֵינוּ מְהֵרָה מִכָּל צָרוֹתֵינוּ, וְנָא, אַל תַּצְרִיכֵנוּ יְיָ אֱלֹהֵינוּ, לֹא לִידֵי מַתְּנַת בָּשָׂר וָדָם, וְלֹא לִידֵי הַלְוָאָתָם. כִּי אִם לְיָדְךָ הַמְּלֵאָה, הַפְּתוּחָה, הַקְּדוֹשָׁה וְהָרְחָבָה, שֶׁלֹּא נֵבוֹשׁ וְלֹא נִכָּלֵם לְעוֹלָם וָעֶד:

Rachaym na, Ado-nai, Elo-haynoo, al yisra-ayl a-mecha, v'al y'roosha-la-yim ee-recha, v'al tzee-on mishkan k'vo-decha, v'al malchoot bayt David m'shee-checha, v'al ha-ba-yit ha-gadol v'ha-kadosh she-nikra shim-cha alav. Elo-haynoo, aveenoo, r'aynoo, zoo-naynoo, parn'saynoo, v'chal-k'laynoo, v'harvee-chaynoo. V'harvach lanoo, Ado-nai, Elo-haynoo, m'hayra meekol tzaro-taynoo. V'na al tatz-ree-chaynoo, Ado-nai, Elo-haynoo, lo lee-day mat'nat basar vadam, v'lo leeday halva-a-tam, kee im l'yad'cha ha-m'lay-a, ha-p'toocha, ha-k'dosha, v'har'chava, shelo nayvosh v'lo neeka-laym l'olam va-ed.

Have mercy, Lord, our God, on Israel your people, and on Jerusalem your city, and on Zion the dwelling-place of Your glory, and on the dynasty of the house of David, Your anointed, and on the great and holy house upon which Your Name is called. Our God, our Father, tend us, feed us, support us and maintain us, and grant us relief. Relieve us, Lord, our God, quickly from all our troubles. And please do not make us dependent, Lord, our God, upon the gifts of flesh and blood nor upon their loans, but only upon Your full, open, holy, and ample hand, so that we should not be ashamed or disgraced, forever and ever.

On the Shabbat add the following paragraph in parentheses.

(רְצֵה וְהַחֲלִיצֵנוּ יְיָ אֱלֹהֵינוּ בְּמִצְוֹתֶיךָ וּבְמִצְוַת יוֹם הַשְּׁבִיעִי הַשַּׁבָּת
הַגָּדוֹל וְהַקָּדוֹשׁ הַזֶּה. כִּי יוֹם זֶה גָּדוֹל וְקָדוֹשׁ הוּא לְפָנֶיךָ, לִשְׁבָּת בּוֹ
וְלָנוּחַ בּוֹ בְּאַהֲבָה כְּמִצְוַת רְצוֹנֶךָ וּבִרְצוֹנְךָ הָנִיחַ לָנוּ יְיָ אֱלֹהֵינוּ, שֶׁלֹּא
תְהֵא צָרָה וְיָגוֹן וַאֲנָחָה בְּיוֹם מְנוּחָתֵנוּ. וְהַרְאֵנוּ יְיָ אֱלֹהֵינוּ בְּנֶחָמַת צִיּוֹן
עִירֶךָ, וּבְבִנְיַן יְרוּשָׁלַיִם עִיר קָדְשֶׁךָ, כִּי אַתָּה הוּא בַּעַל הַיְשׁוּעוֹת וּבַעַל
הַנֶּחָמוֹת:)

(R'tzay v'hacha-lee-tzaynoo, Ado-nai, Elo-haynoo, b'mitzvo-techa, oov-mitzvat yom ha-sh'vee-ee, ha-shabbat ha-gadol v'ha-kadosh ha-zeh. Kee yom zeh gadol v'kadosh hoo l'fa-necha, lishbat bo v'la-noo-ach bo, b'a-havah, k'mitzvat r'tzo-necha. Ooveer-tzon'cha, ha-nee-ach la-noo, Ado-nai, Elo-haynoo, shelo t'hay tzarah v'ya-gon va-anacha b'yom m'noo-cha-taynoo. V'har-aynoo, Ado-nai, Elo-haynoo, b'nechamat tzee-on ee-recha, oov'vinyan y'roosha-la-yim eer kod-shecha, kee atah hoo ba-al ha-y'shoo-ot oova-al ha-nechamot.)

(Favor us and strengthen us, Lord, our God, through Your commandments, and with the commandment of the seventh day, this great and holy Sabbath. For this day is great and holy before You, to refrain from work and to rest on this day, with love, following the command of Your desire. And may it be Your will, to grant us rest, Lord, our God, so that there should be no trouble or sorrow or sighing on Your day of rest. Show us, Lord, our God, the comfort of Zion, Your city, and the building of Jerusalem, the city of Your holiness, for You are the Master of salvation and the Master of consolations.)

אֱלֹהֵינוּ וֵאלֹהֵי אֲבוֹתֵינוּ, יַעֲלֶה וְיָבֹא וְיַגִּיעַ, וְיֵרָאֶה, וְיֵרָצֶה, וְיִשָּׁמַע,
וְיִפָּקֵד, וְיִזָּכֵר זִכְרוֹנֵנוּ וּפִקְדוֹנֵנוּ, וְזִכְרוֹן אֲבוֹתֵינוּ, וְזִכְרוֹן מָשִׁיחַ בֶּן דָּוִד
עַבְדֶּךָ, וְזִכְרוֹן יְרוּשָׁלַיִם עִיר קָדְשֶׁךָ, וְזִכְרוֹן כָּל עַמְּךָ בֵּית יִשְׂרָאֵל
לְפָנֶיךָ, לִפְלֵיטָה לְטוֹבָה לְחֵן וּלְחֶסֶד וּלְרַחֲמִים, לְחַיִּים וּלְשָׁלוֹם בְּיוֹם
חַג הַמַּצּוֹת הַזֶּה. זָכְרֵנוּ יְיָ אֱלֹהֵינוּ בּוֹ לְטוֹבָה. וּפָקְדֵנוּ בוֹ לִבְרָכָה.
וְהוֹשִׁיעֵנוּ בוֹ לְחַיִּים, וּבִדְבַר יְשׁוּעָה וְרַחֲמִים, חוּס וְחָנֵּנוּ, וְרַחֵם עָלֵינוּ
וְהוֹשִׁיעֵנוּ, כִּי אֵלֶיךָ עֵינֵינוּ, כִּי אֵל מֶלֶךְ חַנּוּן וְרַחוּם אָתָּה:

Elo-haynoo vaylo-hay avotaynoo, ya-aleh, v'yavo, v'yagee-a, v'yayra-eh, v'yayra-tzeh, v'yee-shama, v'yee-pakayd, v'yee-zachayr zichro-naynoo oofik-do-naynoo, v'zichron avotaynoo, v'zichron mashee-ach ben Da-vid av-decha, v'zichron y'roosha-la-yim eer kad-shecha, v'zichron kal am'cha bayt yisra-ayl l'fa-necha lif-layta, l'tovah, l'chayn, ool-che-sed, ool-ra-chamim, l'cha-yim ool'shalom b'yom chag ha-mat-zot ha-zeh. Zach-raynoo, Ado-nai, Elo-haynoo, bo l'tovah, oofak-daynoo vo liv-racha, v'hoshee-aynoo vo l'cha-yim. Oovid-var y'shoo-a v'ra-chamim, choos v'cha-naynoo, v'rachaym alaynoo v'hoshee-aynoo, kee ay-lecha ay-naynoo, kee Ayl melech chanoon v'rachoom atah.

Our God and the God of our fathers, may the remembrance and consideration of us, and the remembrance of our fathers, and the remembrance of the anointed son of David, Your servant, and the remembrance of Jerusalem, the city of Your holiness, and the remembrance of Your entire nation, the House of Israel, ascend, approach, reach, appear, be heard, be considered, and be remembered before you for deliverance, for good, for favor, for kindness, and for mercy, for life and for peace on this day of the holiday of Matzot. Remember us on this day, Lord, our God, for good, consider us upon it for blessing, and save us upon it for life. Through the promise of salvation and mercy, spare and favor us, have mercy on us and save us, for our eyes are turned to You, for You are a gracious and merciful God and King.

וּבְנֵה יְרוּשָׁלַיִם עִיר הַקֹּדֶשׁ בִּמְהֵרָה בְיָמֵינוּ. בָּרוּךְ אַתָּה יְיָ, בּוֹנֵה בְּרַחֲמָיו יְרוּשָׁלָיִם. אָמֵן.

Oov-nay y'roosha-la-yim, eer ha-ko-desh, bim-hayra v'ya-maynoo. Baruch atah, Ado-nai, bonay b'ra-chamav y'roosha-la-yim. Amayn.

Rebuild Jerusalem, the holy city, speedily in our days. Blessed are You, Lord, Who rebuilds Jerusalem in His mercy. Amen.

בָּרוּךְ אַתָּה יְיָ אֱלֹהֵינוּ מֶלֶךְ הָעוֹלָם, הָאֵל אָבִינוּ, מַלְכֵּנוּ, אַדִּירֵנוּ בּוֹרְאֵנוּ, גּוֹאֲלֵנוּ, יוֹצְרֵנוּ, קְדוֹשֵׁנוּ קְדוֹשׁ יַעֲקֹב, רוֹעֵנוּ רוֹעֵה יִשְׂרָאֵל. הַמֶּלֶךְ הַטּוֹב, וְהַמֵּטִיב לַכֹּל, שֶׁבְּכָל יוֹם וָיוֹם הוּא הֵטִיב, הוּא מֵטִיב, הוּא יֵיטִיב לָנוּ. הוּא גְמָלָנוּ, הוּא גוֹמְלֵנוּ, הוּא יִגְמְלֵנוּ לָעַד לְחֵן וּלְחֶסֶד וּלְרַחֲמִים וּלְרֶוַח הַצָּלָה וְהַצְלָחָה בְּרָכָה וִישׁוּעָה, נֶחָמָה, פַּרְנָסָה וְכַלְכָּלָה, וְרַחֲמִים, וְחַיִּים וְשָׁלוֹם, וְכָל טוֹב, וּמִכָּל טוּב לְעוֹלָם אַל יְחַסְּרֵנוּ:

Baruch atah, Ado-nai, Elo-haynoo, melech ha-olam, ha-Ayl aveenoo, malkaynoo, adee-raynoo, bor'aynoo, go-alaynoo, yotz'raynoo, k'doshay-noo, k'dosh Ya-akov, ro-aynoo, ro-ay yisra'ayl, ha-melech ha-tov v'hamay-tiv lakol. Sheb'chol yom va-yom hoo haytiv, hoo maytiv, hoo yaytiv la-noo. Hoo g'ma-lanoo, hoo gom'laynoo, hoo yig-m'laynoo la-ad, l'chayn, ool-che-sed, ool-ra-chamim, ool-revach hatzalah, v'hatz-lacha, b'racha, veeshoo-a, nechamah, par-nasah, v'chal-kalah, v'ra-chamim, v'cha-yim, v'shalom v'chol tov. Oo-meekol toov l'olam al y'chas-raynoo.

Blessed are You, Lord, our God, King of the universe, the God of our fathers, our King, our Sovereign, our Creator, our Redeemer, our Maker, our Holy One, the Holy One of Jacob, our Shepherd, the Shepherd of Israel, the good King Who does good for all. Every single day He has done good, He does good, and He will do good for us. He has bestowed, He bestows, and He will bestow benefits upon us forever, with favor, kindness, mercy, and the relief of deliverance, suc-cess, blessing, salvation, comfort, suste-nance and support, mercy, life, peace and all goodness. May You never deprive us of anything good.

הָרַחֲמָן, הוּא יִמְלוֹךְ עָלֵינוּ לְעוֹלָם וָעֶד. הָרַחֲמָן, הוּא יִתְבָּרַךְ בַּשָּׁמַיִם וּבָאָרֶץ. הָרַחֲמָן, הוּא יִשְׁתַּבַּח לְדוֹר דּוֹרִים, וְיִתְפָּאַר בָּנוּ לָעַד וּלְנֵצַח נְצָחִים, וְיִתְהַדַּר בָּנוּ לָעַד וּלְעוֹלְמֵי עוֹלָמִים. הָרַחֲמָן, הוּא יְפַרְנְסֵנוּ בְּכָבוֹד. הָרַחֲמָן, הוּא יִשְׁבּוֹר עָלֵנוּ מֵעַל צַוָּארֵנוּ וְהוּא יוֹלִיכֵנוּ קוֹמְמִיּוּת לְאַרְצֵנוּ. הָרַחֲמָן, הוּא יִשְׁלַח לָנוּ בְּרָכָה מְרֻבָּה בַּבַּיִת הַזֶּה, וְעַל שֻׁלְחָן זֶה שֶׁאָכַלְנוּ עָלָיו. הָרַחֲמָן, הוּא יִשְׁלַח לָנוּ אֶת אֵלִיָּהוּ הַנָּבִיא זָכוּר לַטּוֹב, וִיבַשֶּׂר לָנוּ בְּשׂוֹרוֹת טוֹבוֹת יְשׁוּעוֹת וְנֶחָמוֹת.

Hara-chaman hoo yimloch alaynoo l'olam va-ed. Hara-chaman hoo yit-barach ba-shama-yim oova-aretz. Hara-chaman hoo yishtabach l'dor dorim, v'yit-pa-ar ba-noo la-ad ool-naytzach n'tzachim, v'yit-hadar ba-noo la-ad ool-ol'may olamim. Hara-chaman hoo y'farn'saynoo b'chavod. Hara-chaman hoo yishbor oolaynoo may-al tzava-raynoo v'hoo

May the Merciful One reign over us forever and ever. May the Merciful One be blessed in heaven and on earth. May the Merciful One be praised in every generation, and be glorified through us forever and ever, and be honored through us for all eternity. May the Merciful One support us in honor. May the Merciful One break our yoke off our necks and lead us upright into our

yolee-chaynoo kom'mee-oot l'ar-tzay-noo. Hara-chaman hoo yishlach la-noo b'racha m'roobah baba-yit ha-zeh v'al shoolchan zeh she-achalnoo alav. Hara-chaman hoo yishlach la-noo et Aylee-yahoo ha-navee, zachoor la-tov, veeva-ser la-noo b'sorot tovot, y'shoo-ot, v'nechamot.

land. May the Merciful One send a bountiful blessing in this household and upon this table upon which we have eaten. May the Merciful One send us Elijah the prophet, who is remembered for good, and may he bring us good tidings, salvations, and consolations.

When at one's parents' table, recite the following:

הָרַחֲמָן, הוּא יְבָרֵךְ אֶת אָבִי מוֹרִי בַּעַל הַבַּיִת הַזֶּה, וְאֶת אִמִּי מוֹרָתִי בַּעֲלַת הַבַּיִת הַזֶּה,

Hara-chaman hoo y'va-raych et avee, moree, ba-al haba-yit ha-zeh, v'et eemee, mora-tee, ba-alat haba-yit ha-zeh.

May the Merciful One bless my father, my teacher, the master of this house, and my mother, my teacher, the lady of this house.

When at one's own table, recite the following:

הָרַחֲמָן, הוּא יְבָרֵךְ אוֹתִי (וְאֶת אִשְׁתִּי\בַּעֲלִי וְאֶת וְזַרְעִי) וְאֶת כָּל אֲשֶׁר לִי

Hara-chaman hoo y'va-raych otee (v'et ishtee/ba-alee, v'et zaree) v'et kol asher lee.

May the Merciful One bless me (and my wife/husband, my children) and all that I have.

When at another's table, recite the following:

הָרַחֲמָן, הוּא יְבָרֵךְ אֶת בַּעַל הַבַּיִת הַזֶּה, וְאֶת אִשְׁתּוֹ בַּעֲלַת הַבַּיִת הַזֶּה.

Hara-chaman hoo y'va-raych et ba-al haba-yit ha-zeh v'et ishto, ba-alat haba-yit ha-zeh.

May the Merciful One bless the master of this house and his wife, the lady of this house;

59

אוֹתָם וְאֶת בֵּיתָם וְאֶת זַרְעָם וְאֶת כָּל אֲשֶׁר לָהֶם, אוֹתָנוּ וְאֶת כָּל
אֲשֶׁר לָנוּ, כְּמוֹ שֶׁנִּתְבָּרְכוּ אֲבוֹתֵינוּ, אַבְרָהָם יִצְחָק וְיַעֲקֹב: בַּכֹּל, מִכֹּל,
כֹּל. כֵּן יְבָרֵךְ אוֹתָנוּ כֻּלָּנוּ יַחַד. בִּבְרָכָה שְׁלֵמָה, וְנֹאמַר אָמֵן:

...otam, v'et bay-tam, v'et zaram, v'et kol asher la-hem, ota-noo, v'et kol asher lanoo, k'mo shenit-bar'choo avotaynoo, Avraham, Yitzchak, v'Ya-akov, ba-kol, meekol, kol. Kayn y'va-raych otanoo koo-lanoo yachad biv-racha sh'layma. V'nomar, amayn.

...all of those (participating in this meal), their households, their children, and all that they have, us and all that we have, just as our forefathers, Abraham, Isaac, and Jacob, were blessed in all things, from all things and with all things. So may He bless us all together with a complete blessing. Let us all say, Amen.

בַּמָּרוֹם יְלַמְּדוּ עֲלֵיהֶם וְעָלֵינוּ זְכוּת, שֶׁתְּהֵא לְמִשְׁמֶרֶת שָׁלוֹם, וְנִשָּׂא
בְרָכָה מֵאֵת יְיָ וּצְדָקָה מֵאֱלֹהֵי יִשְׁעֵנוּ, וְנִמְצָא חֵן וְשֵׂכֶל טוֹב בְּעֵינֵי
אֱלֹהִים וְאָדָם:

Ba-marom, y'lam'doo alay-hem v'alaynoo z'choot shet'hay l'mish-meret shalom, v'neesa v'racha may-ayt Ado-nai ootz-dakah may-Elo-hay yish-aynoo, v'nimtza chayn v'say-chel tov b'aynay Elo-him v'adam.

In heaven, may they plead our merits for a lasting peace, and may we receive a blessing from the Lord and justice from the God of our salvation, and may we find favor and good understanding in the eyes of God and man.

On Shabbat, add the sentence in parentheses:

(הָרַחֲמָן, הוּא יַנְחִילֵנוּ יוֹם שֶׁכֻּלּוֹ שַׁבָּת וּמְנוּחָה לְחַיֵּי הָעוֹלָמִים.)

(Hara-chaman hoo yan-chee-laynoo yom shekoolo shabbat oom-noocha l'cha-yay ha-olamim.)

(May the Merciful One cause us to inherit the day that will be entirely one of Shabbat and rest for eternal life.)

הָרַחֲמָן, הוּא יַנְחִילֵנוּ יוֹם שֶׁכֻּלּוֹ טוֹב.

Hara-chaman hoo yan-chee-laynoo yom shekoolo tov.

May the Merciful One cause us to inherit a day of complete goodness.

הָרַחֲמָן, הוּא יְזַכֵּנוּ לִימוֹת הַמָּשִׁיחַ וּלְחַיֵּי הָעוֹלָם הַבָּא.

Hara-chaman hoo y'za-kaynoo leemot hamashee-ach ool-cha-yay ha-olam haba.

May the Merciful One grant us the merit of living in the days of the Messiah and the life of the World-to-Come.

מִגְדּוֹל יְשׁוּעוֹת מַלְכּוֹ, וְעֹשֶׂה חֶסֶד לִמְשִׁיחוֹ לְדָוִד וּלְזַרְעוֹ עַד עוֹלָם: עֹשֶׂה שָׁלוֹם בִּמְרוֹמָיו, הוּא יַעֲשֶׂה שָׁלוֹם, עָלֵינוּ וְעַל כָּל יִשְׂרָאֵל, וְאִמְרוּ אָמֵן:

Migdol y'shoo-ot malko v'o-seh che-sed lim-sheecho, l'Da-vid ool-zaro ad olam. Oseh shalom bim'romav hoo ya-aseh shalom alaynoo v'al kol yisra-ayl, v'imroo, amayn.

He is a tower of salvation to His king and shows kindness to His anointed, to David and to his descendants forever. He who makes peace in the heavens will make peace for us and all of Israel, say, Amen.

יְראוּ אֶת יְיָ קְדֹשָׁיו, כִּי אֵין מַחְסוֹר לִירֵאָיו: כְּפִירִים רָשׁוּ וְרָעֵבוּ, וְדֹרְשֵׁי יְיָ לֹא יַחְסְרוּ כָל טוֹב: הוֹדוּ לַיְיָ כִּי טוֹב, כִּי לְעוֹלָם חַסְדּוֹ: פּוֹתֵחַ אֶת יָדֶךָ, וּמַשְׂבִּיעַ לְכָל חַי רָצוֹן: בָּרוּךְ הַגֶּבֶר אֲשֶׁר יִבְטַח בַּיְיָ, וְהָיָה יְיָ מִבְטַחוֹ: נַעַר הָיִיתִי גַּם זָקַנְתִּי וְלֹא רָאִיתִי צַדִּיק נֶעֱזָב, וְזַרְעוֹ מְבַקֶּשׁ לָחֶם: יְיָ עֹז לְעַמּוֹ יִתֵּן, יְיָ יְבָרֵךְ אֶת עַמּוֹ בַשָּׁלוֹם:

Y'roo et Ado-nai, k'doshav, kee ayn machsor leeray-av. K'feerim rashoo v'ra-ayvoo, v'dor'shay Ado-nai lo yach-s'roo kol tov. Hodoo lado-nai kee tov – kee l'olam chas-do. Potay-ach et ya-decha oomas-bee-a l'chol chai ratzon. Baruch ha-gever asher yivtach bado-nai v'ha-yah Ado-nai mivtacho. Na-ar ha-yeetee, gam zakantee, v'lo ra-eetee tzadik ne-ezav v'zar-o m'va-kesh la-chem. Ado-nai oz l'amo yeetayn; Ado-nai y'va-raych et amo va-shalom.

Fear the Lord—you—His holy ones, for nothing is lacking to those who fear Him. Young lions go poor and hungry, but those who seek the Lord will not be deprived of any good. Give thanks to the Lord for He is good—His kindness endures forever. You open Your hand and satisfy the desire of every living thing. Blessed is the man who trusts in the Lord and for whom the Lord is his support. I was young, and now I have grown old, and I have never seen a righteous man abandoned or his descendants begging for bread. The Lord will give strength to His nation; the Lord will bless His nation with peace.

While reclining on our left side, we recite the following blessing and drink the third cup of wine.

בָּרוּךְ אַתָּה יְיָ, אֱלֹהֵינוּ מֶלֶךְ הָעוֹלָם, בּוֹרֵא פְּרִי הַגָּפֶן:

Baruch atah, Ado-nai, Elo-haynoo, melech ha-olam, boray p'ree haga-fen.

Blessed are you, Lord, our God, King of the universe, Who created the fruit of the vine.

We pour the fourth cup of wine and an extra cup for Elijah the Prophet.
The front door is opened and we recite the following:

שְׁפֹךְ חֲמָתְךָ אֶל־הַגּוֹיִם, אֲשֶׁר לֹא יְדָעוּךָ וְעַל־מַמְלָכוֹת אֲשֶׁר בְּשִׁמְךָ
לֹא קָרָאוּ: כִּי אָכַל אֶת־יַעֲקֹב. וְאֶת־נָוֵהוּ הֵשַׁמּוּ: שְׁפָךְ־עֲלֵיהֶם זַעֲמֶךָ,
וַחֲרוֹן אַפְּךָ יַשִּׂיגֵם: תִּרְדֹּף בְּאַף וְתַשְׁמִידֵם, מִתַּחַת שְׁמֵי יְיָ:

Sh'foch chamat'cha el ha-go-yim asher lo y'da-oocha v'al mamlachot asher b'shim-cha lo kara-oo. Kee achal et Ya-akov v'et na-vayhoo hayshamoo. Sh'fach alayhem za-mecha, vacharon ap'cha ya-see-gaym. Teerdof b'af v'tashmeedaym meetachat sh'may Ado-nai.

Pour out Your wrath on the nations that do not know You and upon the kingdoms that did not call out in Your name. For they devoured Jacob and made his dwelling desolate. Pour Your fury on them, and may Your burning wrath overtake them. Pursue them with fury and destroy them from under the heavens of the Lord.

The door is now closed.

At the moment the door of every home is opened to welcome the prophet Elijah, the room fills with mystery and hope, for freedom and, ultimately, for salvation.

The prophet Elijah–known in Hebrew as Eliyahu–lived when Ahab was king of Israel around the 9th century (BCE). He is a much loved prophet and has frequently been mentioned as the harbinger of the Messiah and as the great problem-solver of Jewish legal and ethical questions.

In fact, calling this fifth cup of wine, placed in the center of the table, Eliyahu's cup, has a multitude of meanings. Symbolically, it is available for any unexpected guest, particularly a disadvantaged one. In addition, the cup resolves an old Talmudic dispute which questioned whether four or five cups of wine should be drunk at the seder.

☙ הלל ☙

Hallel
Recite psalms of praise

After our lavish dinner and expression of gratitude for our food we begin the second part of the Haggadah. We say Hallel, the traditional effusive twenty-six lines of praise to God for His enduring mercy.

Hallel is a group of Psalms that express thanks and praise to God. They form an essential part of the Haggadah recitation, as their content relates powerfully to the miracles of the Exodus.

לֹא לָנוּ יְיָ לֹא לָנוּ כִּי לְשִׁמְךָ תֵּן כָּבוֹד, עַל חַסְדְּךָ עַל אֲמִתֶּךָ. לָמָּה יֹאמְרוּ הַגּוֹיִם, אַיֵּה נָא אֱלֹהֵיהֶם. וֵאלֹהֵינוּ בַשָּׁמָיִם כֹּל אֲשֶׁר חָפֵץ עָשָׂה. עֲצַבֵּיהֶם כֶּסֶף וְזָהָב, מַעֲשֵׂה יְדֵי אָדָם. פֶּה לָהֶם וְלֹא יְדַבֵּרוּ, עֵינַיִם לָהֶם וְלֹא יִרְאוּ. אָזְנַיִם לָהֶם וְלֹא יִשְׁמָעוּ, אַף לָהֶם וְלֹא יְרִיחוּן. יְדֵיהֶם וְלֹא יְמִישׁוּן, רַגְלֵיהֶם וְלֹא יְהַלֵּכוּ, לֹא יֶהְגּוּ בִּגְרוֹנָם. כְּמוֹהֶם יִהְיוּ עֹשֵׂיהֶם, כֹּל אֲשֶׁר בֹּטֵחַ בָּהֶם: יִשְׂרָאֵל בְּטַח בַּיְיָ, עֶזְרָם וּמָגִנָּם הוּא. בֵּית אַהֲרֹן בִּטְחוּ בַיְיָ, עֶזְרָם וּמָגִנָּם הוּא. יִרְאֵי יְיָ בִּטְחוּ בַיְיָ, עֶזְרָם וּמָגִנָּם הוּא:

Lo la-noo, Ado-nai, lo la-noo, kee l'shim-cha tayn kavod, al chas-d'cha al amee-techa. Lamah yom'roo ha-go-yim, A-yay na elo-hayhem? Vay-lo-haynoo va-sha-ma-yim; kol asher cha-faytz, asah. Atza-bayhem kessef v'zahav, ma'assay y'day adam. Peh la-hem v'lo y'da-bayroo; ayna-yim la-hem v'lo yeer-oo. Azna-yim la-hem v'lo yishma-oo; af la-hem v'lo y'reechoon. Y'dayhem —

Not for us, O Lord, not for us, but for Your name give honor, for Your kindness and for Your truthfulness. Why should the nations say, "Where is your God now?" But our God is in heaven; whatever He wishes, He does. Their idols are silver and gold, the handiwork of man. They have a mouth but they do not speak; they have eyes but they do not see. They have ears but they do not hear; they have a nose but they do not smell. Their hands are there—but

v'lo y'meeshoon; raglayhem – v'lo y'ha-laychoo; lo ye-hegoo bigronam. K'mo-hem yi-h'yoo osay-hem, kol asher botay-ach ba-hem. Yisra-ayl, b'tach bado-nai; ezram ooma-geenam hoo. Bayt a-haron, bit-choo vado-nai; ez-ram ooma-geenam hoo. Yeer-ay Ado-nai, bit-choo vado-nai; ezram ooma-geenam hoo.

they do not feel; their feet are there—but they do not walk; they do not murmur with their throat. Like them shall be those who make them, all who trust in them. Israel, trust in the Lord; He is their help and their shield. House of Aaron, trust in the Lord; He is their help and their shield. Those who fear the Lord, trust in the Lord; He is their help and their shield.

יְיָ זְכָרָנוּ יְבָרֵךְ, יְבָרֵךְ אֶת בֵּית יִשְׂרָאֵל, יְבָרֵךְ אֶת בֵּית אַהֲרֹן. יְבָרֵךְ יִרְאֵי יְיָ, הַקְּטַנִּים עִם הַגְּדֹלִים. יֹסֵף יְיָ עֲלֵיכֶם, עֲלֵיכֶם וְעַל בְּנֵיכֶם. בְּרוּכִים אַתֶּם לַיְיָ, עֹשֵׂה שָׁמַיִם וָאָרֶץ. הַשָּׁמַיִם שָׁמַיִם לַיְיָ, וְהָאָרֶץ נָתַן לִבְנֵי אָדָם. לֹא הַמֵּתִים יְהַלְלוּ יָהּ, וְלֹא כָּל יֹרְדֵי דוּמָה. וַאֲנַחְנוּ נְבָרֵךְ יָהּ, מֵעַתָּה וְעַד עוֹלָם, הַלְלוּיָהּ:

Ado-nai, z'cha-ranoo, y'va-raych – y'va-raych et bayt yisra-ayl; y'va-raych et bayt a-haron. Y'va-raych yeer-ay Ado-nai, hak'ta-nim im ha-g'dolim. Yosayf Ado-nai alaychem, alaychem v'al b'nay-chem. B'roo-chim a-tem lado-nai, osay sha-ma-yim va-aretz. Ha-sha-ma-yim sha-ma-yim lado-nai, v'ha-aretz natan liv-nay adam. Lo ha-maytim y'hal'loo Yah, v'lo kol yor'day doom-ah. Va-anachnoo n'va-raych Yah may-atah v'ad olam! Hal'loo-yah!

The Lord, Who remembered us, will bless—He will bless the house of Israel; He will bless the house of Aaron. He will bless those who fear the Lord, the small togeth-er with the great. May the Lord add upon you, upon you and upon your children. Blessed are you to the Lord, the Maker of heaven and earth. The heavens are heav-ens of the Lord, but the earth He gave to the children of men. Neither will the dead praise God, nor all those who descend to the grave. But we shall bless God from now until everlasting! Hallelujah!

אָהַבְתִּי כִּי יִשְׁמַע יְיָ, אֶת קוֹלִי תַּחֲנוּנָי. כִּי הִטָּה אָזְנוֹ לִי וּבְיָמַי אֶקְרָא: אֲפָפוּנִי חֶבְלֵי מָוֶת, וּמְצָרֵי שְׁאוֹל מְצָאוּנִי צָרָה וְיָגוֹן אֶמְצָא. וּבְשֵׁם יְיָ אֶקְרָא, אָנָּה יְיָ מַלְּטָה נַפְשִׁי. חַנּוּן יְיָ וְצַדִּיק, וֵאלֹהֵינוּ מְרַחֵם. שֹׁמֵר פְּתָאיִם יְיָ דַּלּוֹתִי וְלִי יְהוֹשִׁיעַ. שׁוּבִי נַפְשִׁי לִמְנוּחָיְכִי, כִּי יְיָ גָּמַל

עָלָיְכִי. כִּי חִלַּצְתָּ נַפְשִׁי מִמָּוֶת אֶת עֵינִי מִן דִּמְעָה, אֶת רַגְלִי מִדֶּחִי. אֶתְהַלֵּךְ לִפְנֵי יְיָ, בְּאַרְצוֹת הַחַיִּים. הֶאֱמַנְתִּי כִּי אֲדַבֵּר, אֲנִי עָנִיתִי מְאֹד. אֲנִי אָמַרְתִּי בְחָפְזִי כָּל הָאָדָם כֹּזֵב.

Ahavtee kee yishma Ado-nai et kolee ta-chanoo-nai. Kee heetah azno lee, oov-yamai ekra. Afa-foonee chev-lay ma-vet oom-tza-ray sh'ol m'tza-oonee, tzarah v'ya-gon emtza, oov-shaym Ado-nai ekra, Anah, Ado-nai, mal'tah nafshee! Chanoon Ado-nai v'tzadik, vaylo-haynoo m'ra-chaym. Shomayr p'ta-yim Ado-nai; da-lote, v'lee y'hoshee-a. Shoovee nafshee lim-noo-chai-chee, kee Ado-nai gamal alai-chee. Kee chee-latz-ta nafshee mee-ma-vet, et aynee min dim-ah, et raglee mee-dechee. Et-ha-laych lifnay Ado-nai b'artzot ha-cha-yim. He-emantee kee ada-bayr, A-nee a-neetee m'od, a-nee amartee v'chafzee, Kol ha-adam kozayv.

I wished that the Lord would hear my voice in my supplications. For He extended His ear to me, and I shall call out in my days. When bands of death surrounded me and the boundaries of the grave befell me, and I found trouble and grief, I called out in the name of the Lord, "Please, O Lord, save my soul!" The Lord is gracious and righteous, and our God is merciful. The Lord protects the simple; when I was poor, He saved me. Return my soul to your rest, the Lord has dealt bountifully with you. You freed my soul from death, my eyes from tears, my foot from stumbling. I shall walk before the Lord in the lands of the living. I kept my faith even when I said, "I am suffering deeply," and in my haste I said, "All men are liars."

מָה אָשִׁיב לַיְיָ, כָּל תַּגְמוּלוֹהִי עָלָי. כּוֹס יְשׁוּעוֹת אֶשָּׂא, וּבְשֵׁם יְיָ אֶקְרָא. נְדָרַי לַיְיָ אֲשַׁלֵּם, נֶגְדָה נָּא לְכָל עַמּוֹ. יָקָר בְּעֵינֵי יְיָ הַמָּוְתָה לַחֲסִידָיו. אָנָּה יְיָ כִּי אֲנִי עַבְדֶּךָ, אֲנִי עַבְדְּךָ, בֶּן אֲמָתֶךָ פִּתַּחְתָּ לְמוֹסֵרָי. לְךָ אֶזְבַּח זֶבַח תּוֹדָה וּבְשֵׁם יְיָ אֶקְרָא. נְדָרַי לַיְיָ אֲשַׁלֵּם, נֶגְדָה נָּא לְכָל עַמּוֹ. בְּחַצְרוֹת בֵּית יְיָ בְּתוֹכֵכִי יְרוּשָׁלָיִם הַלְלוּיָהּ.

Mah ashiv lado-nai kol tagmoolo-hee a-lai? Kos y'shoo-ot essa, oov-shaym Ado-nai ekra. N'da-rai lado-nai asha-laym negdah na l'chol amo. Yakar b'aynay Ado-nai ha-mavtah la-chaseedav. Anah,

How can I repay the Lord for all His favors toward me? I shall lift up a cup of salvations, and I shall call out in the name of the Lord. I shall pay my vows to the Lord in the presence of all His people. Precious in the eyes of the Lord is the

Ado-nai, kee a-nee avdecha – a-nee avd'cha ben ama-techa – peetach-ta l'mosay-rai. L'cha ezbach ze-vach todah, oov-shaym Ado-nai ekrah. N'da-rai lado-nai asha-laym negdah nah l'chol amo, b'chatz-rot bayt Ado-nai, b'tochaychee, y'roo-shala-yim. Hal'loo-yah!

death of His pious ones. Please, O Lord, for I am Your servant—I am Your servant the son of Your maidservant—You have loosened my bonds. To You I shall slaughter a thanksgiving offering, and I shall call out in the name of the Lord. I shall pay my vows to the Lord now in the presence of all His people, in the courtyards of the Lord's house, in your midst, O Jerusalem. Hallelujah!

הַלְלוּ אֶת יְיָ, כָּל גּוֹיִם, שַׁבְּחוּהוּ כָּל הָאֻמִּים. כִּי גָבַר עָלֵינוּ חַסְדּוֹ, וֶאֱמֶת יְיָ לְעוֹלָם הַלְלוּיָהּ:

Hal'loo et Ado-nai, kol go-yim. Shab'choohoo, kol ha-oomim. Kee ga-var alaynoo chasdo, ve-emet Ado-nai l'olam. Hal'loo-yah!

Praise the Lord, all nations. Laud Him, all peoples. His kindness has overwhelmed us, and the truth of the Lord is eternal. Hallelujah!

הוֹדוּ לַיְיָ כִּי טוֹב, כִּי לְעוֹלָם חַסְדּוֹ:
יֹאמַר נָא יִשְׂרָאֵל, כִּי לְעוֹלָם חַסְדּוֹ:
יֹאמְרוּ נָא בֵית אַהֲרֹן, כִּי לְעוֹלָם חַסְדּוֹ:
יֹאמְרוּ נָא יִרְאֵי יְיָ, כִּי לְעוֹלָם חַסְדּוֹ:

Hodoo lado-nai kee tov, kee l'o-lam chasdo.

Yomar na yisra-ayl, Kee l'olam chasdo.

Yom'roo na vayt a-haron, Kee l'o-lam chasdo.

Yom'roo na yir-ay Ado-nai, Kee l'olam chasdo.

Give thanks to the Lord because He is good, for His kindness is eternal.

Let Israel shall now say, "For His kindness is eternal."

Let the house of Aaron say, "For His kindness is eternal."

Let those who fear the Lord say, "For His kindness is eternal."

מִן הַמֵּצַר קָרָאתִי יָּהּ, עָנָנִי בַמֶּרְחָב יָהּ. יְיָ לִי לֹא אִירָא, מַה יַּעֲשֶׂה לִי אָדָם. יְיָ לִי בְּעֹזְרָי, וַאֲנִי אֶרְאֶה בְשֹׂנְאָי. טוֹב לַחֲסוֹת בַּיְיָ, מִבְּטֹחַ בָּאָדָם. טוֹב לַחֲסוֹת בַּיְיָ מִבְּטֹחַ בִּנְדִיבִים. כָּל גּוֹיִם סְבָבוּנִי בְּשֵׁם יְיָ כִּי

אֲמִילַם. סַבּוּנִי גַם סְבָבוּנִי, בְּשֵׁם יְיָ כִּי אֲמִילַם. סַבּוּנִי כִדְבֹרִים דֹּעֲכוּ
כְּאֵשׁ קוֹצִים, בְּשֵׁם יְיָ כִּי אֲמִילַם. דָּחֹה דְחִיתַנִי לִנְפֹּל, וַיְיָ עֲזָרָנִי. עָזִּי
וְזִמְרָת יָהּ, וַיְהִי לִי לִישׁוּעָה. קוֹל רִנָּה וִישׁוּעָה בְּאָהֳלֵי צַדִּיקִים, יְמִין יְיָ
עֹשָׂה חָיִל. יְמִין יְיָ רוֹמֵמָה, יְמִין יְיָ עֹשָׂה חָיִל. לֹא אָמוּת כִּי אֶחְיֶה,
וַאֲסַפֵּר מַעֲשֵׂי יָהּ. יַסֹּר יִסְּרַנִי יָּהּ, וְלַמָּוֶת לֹא נְתָנָנִי. פִּתְחוּ לִי שַׁעֲרֵי
צֶדֶק, אָבֹא בָם אוֹדֶה יָהּ. זֶה הַשַּׁעַר לַיְיָ, צַדִּיקִים יָבֹאוּ בוֹ. אוֹדְךָ כִּי
עֲנִיתָנִי, וַתְּהִי לִי לִישׁוּעָה. אוֹדְךָ כִּי עֲנִיתָנִי וַתְּהִי לִי לִישׁוּעָה. אֶבֶן
מָאֲסוּ הַבּוֹנִים, הָיְתָה לְרֹאשׁ פִּנָּה.   אֶבֶן מָאֲסוּ הַבּוֹנִים, הָיְתָה לְרֹאשׁ
פִּנָּה. מֵאֵת יְיָ הָיְתָה זֹּאת, הִיא נִפְלָאת בְּעֵינֵינוּ:   מֵאֵת יְיָ הָיְתָה זֹּאת,
הִיא נִפְלָאת בְּעֵינֵינוּ. זֶה הַיּוֹם עָשָׂה יְיָ, נָגִילָה וְנִשְׂמְחָה בוֹ. זֶה הַיּוֹם
עָשָׂה יְיָ נָגִילָה וְנִשְׂמְחָה בוֹ.

Min ha-maytzar kara-tee Yah; ana-nee va-merchav Yah. Ado-nai lee; lo eera. Mah ya-asseh lee adam? Ado-nai lee b'ozrai, va-anee er-eh v'son'ai. Tov la-chasot bado-nai mee-b'to-ach ba-adam. Tov la-chasot bado-nai mee-b'to-ach bin-deevim. Kol go-yim s'va-voonee; b'shaym Ado-nai kee amee-lam. Sa-boonee, gam s'va-voonee; b'shaym Ado-nai kee amee-lam. Sa-boonee chid'vo-reem; do-achoo k'aysh ko-tzim; b'shaym Ado-nai kee amee-lam. Da-cho d'chee-tanee linpol, vado-nai aza-ranee. Azee v'zimrat Yah, vay-hee lee leeshoo-a. Kol reenah veeshoo-a b'a-halay tzadeekim: Y'min Ado-nai osah cha-yil. Y'min Ado-nai ro-mayma; y'min Adonai osah cha-yil. Lo amoot kee echyeh va-asa-payr ma-asay Yah. Yassor

In my distress I called God; God answered me with a vast expanse. The Lord is with me; I shall not fear. What can man do to me? The Lord is for me as my helper, and I shall gaze upon them that hate me. It is better to take refuge in the Lord than to trust in man. It is better to take refuge in the Lord than to trust in princes. All nations surround me; in the name of the Lord I shall cut them off. They encircle me, O they surround me; in the name of the Lord I shall cut them off. They encircle me like bees; they are extinguished like a thorn fire; in the name of the Lord I shall cut them off. You pushed me to fall, but the Lord helped me. The Lord is my strength and my song, and He has become my salvation. A voice of singing praises and salvation is in the tents of the righteous: "The right hand of the Lord deals

yis'ranee Yah, v'lama-vet lo n'ta-nanee. Pit'choo lee sha-aray tzedek; avo vam odeh Yah. Zeh ha-sha-ar lado-nai; tzadeekim yavo-oo vo. Od'cha kee anee-tanee, vat'hee lee leeshoo-a. Od'cha kee anee-tanee, vat'hee lee leeshoo-a. Even ma-asoo ha-bonim ha-y'tah l'rosh peenah. Even ma-asoo ha-bonim ha-y'tah l'rosh peenah. May-ayt Ado-nai ha-y'tah zot; hee niflat b'ay-naynoo. May-ayt Ado-nai ha-y'tah zot; hee niflat b'ay-naynoo. Zeh ha-yom asah Ado-nai; nageelah v'nis-m'cha vo. Zeh ha-yom asah Ado-nai; nageelah v'nis-m'cha vo.

valiantly. The right hand of the Lord is exalted; the right hand of the Lord deals valiantly." I shall not die but I shall live and tell the deeds of God. God has chastised me, but He has not delivered me to death. Open for me the gates of righteousness; I shall enter them and thank God. This is the Lord's gate; the righteous will enter therein. I shall thank You because You have answered me, and You have become my salvation. The stone that the builders rejected has become a cornerstone. This is the Lord's doing; it is wondrous in our eyes. This is the day that the Lord made; we shall exalt and rejoice.

אָנָּא יְיָ הוֹשִׁיעָה נָּא׃ אָנָּא יְיָ הוֹשִׁיעָה נָּא׃

אָנָּא יְיָ הַצְלִיחָה נָּא׃ אָנָּא יְיָ הַצְלִיחָה נָּא׃

Ana, Ado-nai, hoshee-a na! Ana, Ado-nai, hoshee-a na!

Ana, Ado-nai, hatzleecha na! Ana, Ado-nai, hatzleecha na!

Please, O Lord, save us now! Please, O Lord, save us now!

Please, O Lord, make us prosperous now! Please, O Lord, make us prosperous now!

בָּרוּךְ הַבָּא בְּשֵׁם יְיָ, בֵּרַכְנוּכֶם מִבֵּית יְיָ. בָּרוּךְ הַבָּא בְּשֵׁם יְיָ, בֵּרַכְנוּכֶם מִבֵּית יְיָ. אֵל יְיָ וַיָּאֶר לָנוּ, אִסְרוּ חַג בַּעֲבֹתִים עַד קַרְנוֹת הַמִּזְבֵּחַ. אֵל יְיָ וַיָּאֶר לָנוּ, אִסְרוּ חַג בַּעֲבֹתִים, עַד קַרְנוֹת הַמִּזְבֵּחַ. אֵלִי אַתָּה וְאוֹדֶךָּ אֱלֹהַי אֲרוֹמְמֶךָּ. אֵלִי אַתָּה וְאוֹדֶךָּ אֱלֹהַי אֲרוֹמְמֶךָּ׃ הוֹדוּ לַיְיָ כִּי טוֹב, כִּי לְעוֹלָם חַסְדּוֹ׃ הוֹדוּ לַיְיָ כִּי טוֹב, כִּי לְעוֹלָם חַסְדּוֹ.

Baruch haba b'shaym Ado-nai; bay-rachnoo-chem mee-bayt Ado-nai. Baruch haba b'shaym Ado-nai; bay-rachnoo-chem mee-bayt Ado-nai. Ayl Ado-nai, va-ya-er la-noo. Is-roo chag ba-

Blessed be he who has come in the name of the Lord; we bless you from the house of the Lord. Blessed be he who has come in the name of the Lord; we bless you from the house of the Lord. The Lord is God, and He gave us light. Bind the sacrifice with ropes

68

avotim ad karnot ha-mizbayach. Ayl Ado-nai, va-ya-er la-noo. Is-roo chag ba-avotim ad karnot ha-mizbayach. Aylee atah v'o-deka; Elo-hai, arom'meka. Aylee atah v'o-deka; Elo-hai, arom'meka. Hodoo lado-nai kee tov, kee l'o-lam chasdo. Hodoo lado-nai kee tov, kee l'olam chasdo.

until it is brought to the corners of the altar. The Lord is God, and He gave us light. Bind the sacrifice with ropes until it is brought to the corners of the altar. You are my God and I shall thank You; the God of my father, and I shall exalt You. You are my God and I shall thank You; the God of my father, and I shall exalt You. Give thanks to the Lord because He is good, for His kindness is eternal. Give thanks to the Lord because He is good, for His kindness is eternal.

יְהַלְלוּךָ יְיָ אֱלֹהֵינוּ כָּל מַעֲשֶׂיךָ, וַחֲסִידֶיךָ צַדִּיקִים עוֹשֵׂי רְצוֹנֶךָ, וְכָל עַמְּךָ בֵּית יִשְׂרָאֵל בְּרִנָּה יוֹדוּ וִיבָרְכוּ וִישַׁבְּחוּ וִיפָאֲרוּ וִירוֹמְמוּ וְיַעֲרִיצוּ וְיַקְדִּישׁוּ וְיַמְלִיכוּ אֶת שִׁמְךָ מַלְכֵּנוּ, כִּי לְךָ טוֹב לְהוֹדוֹת וּלְשִׁמְךָ נָאֶה לְזַמֵּר, כִּי מֵעוֹלָם וְעַד עוֹלָם אַתָּה אֵל.

Y'hal'loocha, Ado-nai, Elo-haynoo, kol ma-a-secha, va-chasee-decha, tzadeekim osay r'tzo-necha, v'chol am'cha, bayt yisra-ayl, b'reenah yodoo, vee-var'choo, vee-shab'choo, vee-fa-aroo, vee-rom'moo, v'ya-areet-zoo, v'yak-deeshoo, v'yam-leechoo et shim-cha, mal-kaynoo, kee l'cha tov l'hodot, ool'shim'cha na-eh l'za-mayr, kee may-olam v'ad olam, atah Ayl.

All Your works will praise You, Lord, our God, and Your pious ones, the righteous who perform Your will, and all Your people, the house of Israel, will joyously give thanks, bless, praise, glorify, extol, exalt, revere, sanctify, and crown Your name, our King, for it is good to thank You, and it is fitting to sing to Your name, for from everlasting to everlasting, You are God.

הוֹדוּ לַיְיָ כִּי טוֹב, כִּי לְעוֹלָם חַסְדּוֹ: הוֹדוּ לֵאלֹהֵי הָאֱלֹהִים, כִּי לְעוֹלָם חַסְדּוֹ: הוֹדוּ לַאֲדֹנֵי הָאֲדֹנִים, כִּי לְעוֹלָם חַסְדּוֹ: לְעֹשֵׂה נִפְלָאוֹת גְּדֹלוֹת לְבַדּוֹ, כִּי לְעוֹלָם חַסְדּוֹ: לְעֹשֵׂה הַשָּׁמַיִם בִּתְבוּנָה, כִּי לְעוֹלָם חַסְדּוֹ: לְרוֹקַע הָאָרֶץ עַל הַמָּיִם, כִּי לְעוֹלָם חַסְדּוֹ: לְעֹשֵׂה אוֹרִים גְּדֹלִים, כִּי לְעוֹלָם חַסְדּוֹ: אֶת הַשֶּׁמֶשׁ לְמֶמְשֶׁלֶת בַּיּוֹם, כִּי לְעוֹלָם חַסְדּוֹ: אֶת

הַיָּרֵחַ וְכוֹכָבִים לְמֶמְשְׁלוֹת בַּלָּיְלָה, כִּי לְעוֹלָם חַסְדּוֹ: לְמַכֵּה מִצְרַיִם בִּבְכוֹרֵיהֶם, כִּי לְעוֹלָם חַסְדּוֹ: וַיּוֹצֵא יִשְׂרָאֵל מִתּוֹכָם, כִּי לְעוֹלָם חַסְדּוֹ: בְּיָד חֲזָקָה וּבִזְרוֹעַ נְטוּיָה, כִּי לְעוֹלָם חַסְדּוֹ: לְגֹזֵר יַם סוּף לִגְזָרִים, כִּי לְעוֹלָם חַסְדּוֹ: וְהֶעֱבִיר יִשְׂרָאֵל בְּתוֹכוֹ, כִּי לְעוֹלָם חַסְדּוֹ: וְנִעֵר פַּרְעֹה וְחֵילוֹ בְיַם סוּף, כִּי לְעוֹלָם חַסְדּוֹ: לְמוֹלִיךְ עַמּוֹ בַּמִּדְבָּר, כִּי לְעוֹלָם חַסְדּוֹ: לְמַכֵּה מְלָכִים גְּדֹלִים, כִּי לְעוֹלָם חַסְדּוֹ: וַיַּהֲרֹג מְלָכִים אַדִּירִים, כִּי לְעוֹלָם חַסְדּוֹ: לְסִיחוֹן מֶלֶךְ הָאֱמֹרִי, כִּי לְעוֹלָם חַסְדּוֹ: וּלְעוֹג מֶלֶךְ הַבָּשָׁן, כִּי לְעוֹלָם חַסְדּוֹ: וְנָתַן אַרְצָם לְנַחֲלָה, כִּי לְעוֹלָם חַסְדּוֹ: נַחֲלָה לְיִשְׂרָאֵל עַבְדּוֹ, כִּי לְעוֹלָם חַסְדּוֹ: שֶׁבְּשִׁפְלֵנוּ זָכַר לָנוּ, כִּי לְעוֹלָם חַסְדּוֹ: וַיִּפְרְקֵנוּ מִצָּרֵינוּ, כִּי לְעוֹלָם חַסְדּוֹ: נוֹתֵן לֶחֶם לְכָל בָּשָׂר, כִּי לְעוֹלָם חַסְדּוֹ: הוֹדוּ לְאֵל הַשָּׁמָיִם, כִּי לְעוֹלָם חַסְדּוֹ:

Hodoo lado-nai kee tov kee l'olam chasdo. Hodoo lay-lohay ha-elo-him, kee l'olam chasdo. Hodoo la-adonay ha-adonim, kee l'olam chas-do. L'osay nifla-ot g'dolot l'vado, kee l'olam chasdo. L'osay ha-shama-yim bitvoona, kee l'olam chasdo. L'roka ha-aretz al ha-ma-yim, kee l'olam chasdo. L'osay orim g'dolim, kee l'o-lam chasdo. Et ha-shemesh l'mem-shelet ba-yom, kee l'olam chasdo. Et ha-yaray-ach v'cho-chavim l'mem-sh'lot ba-lailah, kee l'olam chasdo. L'ma-kay mitzra-yim biv-cho-ray-hem, kee l'olam chasdo. Va-yotzay yisra-ayl mee-tocham, kee l'olam chasdo. B'yad chaza-kah ooviz-ro-a n'too-ya, kee l'olam chasdo. L'go-zayr yam soof lig-zarim, kee l'olam chasdo. V'he-eveer yisra'ayl b'to-cho, kee l'olam chasdo. V'nee-ayr

Give thanks to the Lord for He is good, for His kindness is eternal. Give thanks to the God of the angels, for His kindness is eternal. Give thanks to the Lord of lords, for His kindness is eternal. To Him Who performs great wonders alone, for His kindness is eternal. To Him Who made the heavens with understanding, for His kindness is eternal. To Him Who spread out the earth over the water, for His kindness is eternal. To Him Who made great luminaries, for His kindness is eternal. The sun to rule by day, for His kindness is eternal. The moon and stars to rule by night, for His kindness is eternal. To Him Who struck the Egyptians with their firstborn, for His kindness is eternal. And He took Israel from their midst, for His kindness is eternal. With a strong hand and with an outstretched arm, for His kindness is eternal. To Him Who cut the Sea of Reeds asunder, for His kindness is eternal. And crossed Israel in its midst, for His kindness is eter-

Paroh v'chaylo v'yam soof, kee l'olam chasdo. L'molich amo bamidbar, kee l'olam chasdo. L'ma-kay m'lachim g'dolim, kee l'olam chasdo. Va-ya-harog m'lachim adee-rim, kee l'olam chasdo. L'seechon melech ha-emoree, kee l'olam chasdo. Oo-l'og melech ha-bashan, kee l'olam chasdo. V'natan ar-tzam l'na-chalah, kee l'olam chasdo. Na-chalah l'yisra-ayl, avdo, kee l'olam chasdo. Sheb'shif-laynoo zachar lanoo, kee l'olam chasdo. Va-yifr'kaynoo mee-tza-raynoo, kee l'olam chasdo. Notayn lechem l'chol basar, kee l'olam chasdo. Hodoo l'ayl ha-shama-yim, kee l'olam chasdo.

nal. And threw Pharaoh and his army into the Sea of Reeds, for His kindness is eternal. To Him Who led His people in the desert, for His kindness is eternal. To Him Who struck down great kings, for His kindness is eternal. And slew mighty kings, for His kindness is eternal. Sihon, the king of the Amorites, for His kindness is eternal. And Og, the king of Bashan, for His kindness is eternal. And He gave their land as an inheritance, for His kindness is eternal. An inheritance to Israel, His servant, for His kindness is eternal. Who remembered us in our humble state, for His kindness is eternal. And he rescued us from our adversaries, for His kindness is eternal. Who gives food to all flesh, for His kindness is eternal. Give thanks to the God of heaven, for His kindness is eternal.

נִשְׁמַת כָּל חַי, תְּבָרֵךְ אֶת שִׁמְךָ יְיָ אֱלֹהֵינוּ. וְרוּחַ כָּל בָּשָׂר, תְּפָאֵר וּתְרוֹמֵם זִכְרְךָ מַלְכֵּנוּ תָּמִיד, מִן הָעוֹלָם וְעַד הָעוֹלָם אַתָּה אֵל. וּמִבַּלְעָדֶיךָ אֵין לָנוּ מֶלֶךְ גּוֹאֵל וּמוֹשִׁיעַ, פּוֹדֶה וּמַצִּיל וּמְפַרְנֵס וּמְרַחֵם, בְּכָל עֵת צָרָה וְצוּקָה. אֵין לָנוּ מֶלֶךְ אֶלָּא אָתָּה: אֱלֹהֵי הָרִאשׁוֹנִים וְהָאַחֲרוֹנִים, אֱלוֹהַּ כָּל בְּרִיּוֹת, אֲדוֹן כָּל תּוֹלָדוֹת, הַמְהֻלָּל בְּרֹב הַתִּשְׁבָּחוֹת, הַמְנַהֵג עוֹלָמוֹ בְּחֶסֶד, וּבְרִיּוֹתָיו בְּרַחֲמִים. וַיְיָ לֹא יָנוּם וְלֹא יִישָׁן, הַמְעוֹרֵר יְשֵׁנִים וְהַמֵּקִיץ נִרְדָּמִים, וְהַמֵּשִׂיחַ אִלְּמִים, וְהַמַּתִּיר אֲסוּרִים, וְהַסּוֹמֵךְ נוֹפְלִים, וְהַזּוֹקֵף כְּפוּפִים, לְךָ לְבַדְּךָ אֲנַחְנוּ מוֹדִים. אִלּוּ פִינוּ מָלֵא שִׁירָה כַּיָּם, וּלְשׁוֹנֵנוּ רִנָּה כַּהֲמוֹן גַּלָּיו, וְשִׂפְתוֹתֵינוּ שֶׁבַח כְּמֶרְחֲבֵי רָקִיעַ, וְעֵינֵינוּ מְאִירוֹת כַּשֶּׁמֶשׁ וְכַיָּרֵחַ, וְיָדֵינוּ פְרוּשׂוֹת כְּנִשְׁרֵי שָׁמָיִם, וְרַגְלֵינוּ קַלּוֹת כָּאַיָּלוֹת, אֵין אֲנַחְנוּ מַסְפִּיקִים, לְהוֹדוֹת לְךָ יְיָ אֱלֹהֵינוּ וֵאלֹהֵי אֲבוֹתֵינוּ, וּלְבָרֵךְ אֶת שְׁמֶךָ עַל אַחַת מֵאֶלֶף אֶלֶף אַלְפֵי אֲלָפִים וְרִבֵּי רְבָבוֹת פְּעָמִים, הַטּוֹבוֹת שֶׁעָשִׂיתָ עִם אֲבוֹתֵינוּ וְעִמָּנוּ. מִמִּצְרַיִם גְּאַלְתָּנוּ יְיָ אֱלֹהֵינוּ, וּמִבֵּית עֲבָדִים פְּדִיתָנוּ, בְּרָעָב

‮⁌‬ This beautiful composition was created in the 2nd century BCE, and expresses our absolute love and trust in God, as well as at the recognition that it is impossible for us to ever sufficiently thank and praise God. Nevertheless, we must always use whatever ability we have to try to find a way to express our gratitude.

זַנְתָּנוּ, וּבְשָׂבָע כִּלְכַּלְתָּנוּ, מֵחֶרֶב הִצַּלְתָּנוּ, וּמִדֶּבֶר מִלַּטְתָּנוּ, וּמֵחֳלָיִם
רָעִים וְנֶאֱמָנִים דִּלִּיתָנוּ: עַד הֵנָּה עֲזָרוּנוּ רַחֲמֶיךָ, וְלֹא עֲזָבוּנוּ חֲסָדֶיךָ
וְאַל תִּטְּשֵׁנוּ יְיָ אֱלֹהֵינוּ לָנֶצַח. עַל כֵּן אֵבָרִים שֶׁפִּלַּגְתָּ בָּנוּ, וְרוּחַ וּנְשָׁמָה
שֶׁנָּפַחְתָּ בְּאַפֵּינוּ, וְלָשׁוֹן אֲשֶׁר שַׂמְתָּ בְּפִינוּ, הֵן הֵם יוֹדוּ וִיבָרְכוּ וִישַׁבְּחוּ
וִיפָאֲרוּ וִירוֹמְמוּ וְיַעֲרִיצוּ וְיַקְדִּישׁוּ וְיַמְלִיכוּ אֶת שִׁמְךָ מַלְכֵּנוּ, כִּי כָל פֶּה
לְךָ יוֹדֶה, וְכָל לָשׁוֹן לְךָ תִשָּׁבַע, וְכָל בֶּרֶךְ לְךָ תִכְרַע, וְכָל קוֹמָה
לְפָנֶיךָ תִשְׁתַּחֲוֶה, וְכָל לְבָבוֹת יִירָאוּךָ, וְכָל קֶרֶב וּכְלָיוֹת יְזַמְּרוּ
לִשְׁמֶךָ. כַּדָּבָר שֶׁכָּתוּב, כָּל עַצְמוֹתַי תֹּאמַרְנָה יְיָ מִי כָמוֹךָ. מַצִּיל עָנִי
מֵחָזָק מִמֶּנּוּ, וְעָנִי וְאֶבְיוֹן מִגֹּזְלוֹ: מִי יִדְמֶה לָּךְ, וּמִי יִשְׁוֶה לָּךְ וּמִי יַעֲרָךְ
לָךְ: הָאֵל הַגָּדוֹל הַגִּבּוֹר וְהַנּוֹרָא, אֵל עֶלְיוֹן קֹנֵה שָׁמַיִם וָאָרֶץ: נְהַלֶּלְךָ
וּנְשַׁבֵּחֲךָ וּנְפָאֶרְךָ וּנְבָרֵךְ אֶת־שֵׁם קָדְשֶׁךָ. כָּאָמוּר, לְדָוִד, בָּרְכִי נַפְשִׁי
אֶת יְיָ, וְכָל קְרָבַי אֶת שֵׁם קָדְשׁוֹ:

Nish'mat kol chai t'varaych et shim-cha, Ado-nai, Elo-haynoo, v'roo-ach kol basar t'fa-ayr oot'romaym zichr'cha, mal-kaynoo, tamid. Min ha-olam v'ad ha-olam atah Ayl. Oomee-bal-a-decha ayn lanoo melech go-ayl oomoshee-a, podeh, oo-matzeel, oom-far-nayss oom-rachaym. B'chol ayt tzarah v'tzookah, ayn lanoo melech ela atah. Elo-hay ha-reeshonim v'ha-acharonim, Elo-ah kol b'reeot, adon kol tola-dot, ham'hoo-lal b'rov ha-tishbachot, ham'na-hayg olamo b'che-sed oov-ree-otav b'ra-chamim. Vado-nai lo yanoom v'lo yeeshan. Ham'o-rayr y'shaynim v'ha-maykitz nirdamim, v'ha-maysee-ach eel'mim, v'ha-mateer asoo-rim, v'ha-somaych nof'lim, v'ha-zokayf k'foo-fim. L'cha

The soul of every living thing shall praise Your name, Lord, our God, and the spirit of all flesh shall glorify and forever exalt Your remembrance, our King. From eternity to eternity You are God. Besides You, we have no king Who redeems and saves, ransoms, rescues, sustains and shows mercy. In every time of trouble and distress, We have no king but You. You are God of the first and of the last, God of all creations, Master of all generations, Who is acclaimed with many praises, Who rules His world with kindness and His creatures with mercy. God neither slumbers nor sleeps. He awakens the sleepers and arouses the slumberers, causes the mute to speak, frees the imprisoned, supports the fallen and straightens the bent. To You alone we give thanks. Even if our mouths were

l'vad'cha anachnoo modim. Ee-loo feenoo ma-lay shee-rah ka-yam, ool-sho-naynoo reenah ka-ha-mon galav, v'sif-totaynoo shevach k'mer-chavay rakee-a, v'ay-naynoo m'eerot ka-shemesh v'cha-yaray-ach, v'ya-daynoo f'roosot k'nishray sha-ma-yim, v'rag-laynoo kalot ka-a-yalot, ayn anach-noo maspeekim l'hodot l'cha, Ado-nai, Elo-haynoo vaylo-hay avotaynoo, ool-varaych et sh'mecha al achat may-elef alfay alafim, v'ree-bay r'vavot p'amim ha-tovot she-asee-ta im avotaynoo v'ee-manoo. Mee-mitzra-yim g'al-tanoo, Ado-nai, Elo-haynoo, oomee-bayt avadim p'dee-tanoo. B'ra-av zan-tanoo, oov-sava kil-kal-tanoo. May-cherev heetzal-tanoo, oomee-dever m'lat-tanoo, oomay-chala-yim ra-im v'ne-emanim dee-lee-tanoo. Ad haynah, aza-roonoo racha-mecha, v'lo aza-voonoo chasa-decha. V'al tit'shaynoo, Ado-nai Elo-haynoo, la-netzach. Al kayn, ayvarim shepee-lagta banoo, v'roo-ach oon-shamah she-nafach-ta b'a-paynoo, v'lashon asher samta b'feenoo – hayn haym yodoo, vee-var'choo, vee-shab'choo, vee-fa-aroo, vee-rom'moo, v'ya-areetzoo, v'yak-deeshoo, v'yam-leechoo et shim-cha, mal-kaynoo. Kee chol peh l'cha yodeh, v'chol lashon l'cha tee-shava, v'chol berech l'cha tichra, v'chol komah l'fa-necha tishta-chaveh, v'chol l'vavot yeera-oocha, v'chol

filled with song like the sea, our tongues with rejoicing like the multitude of its waves, our lips with praise like the expanse of the heaven, our eyes as radiant as the sun and the moon, our hands as outspread as the eagles in the sky, and our feet as swift as deer, we could never sufficiently praise You, Lord, our God and the God of our fathers, or bless Your Name for even one of the thousands upon thousands, and myriads upon myriads of the kindnesses that You have done for our fathers and for us. From Egypt You redeemed us, Lord, our God, and from the house of slavery You released us. In famine You fed us, and in plenty You sustained us. From the sword You saved us, and from pestilence You delivered us, and from harsh and serious illnesses You spared us. Until now, Your mercies have helped us, and Your kindnesses have not forsaken us. Do not abandon us, Lord our God, forever. Therefore, the limbs that You formed in us, and the breath and spirit that You blew into our nostrils and the tongues that You placed into our mouths—they themselves will thank, bless, praise, glorify, exalt, revere, sanctify and proclaim the sovereignty of Your Name, our King. For every mouth will thank You, every tongue will swear to You, every knee will bend to You, every being that stands will prostrate itself to You, all hearts will fear You, and all innermost parts will sing to Your name.

kerev ooch-la-yot y'zam'roo lish-mecha. Ka-davar she-katoov, Kol atz-motai tomarnah, Ado-nai, mee chamocha? Matzeel anee may-chazak mee-menoo v'anee v'evyon meegoz'-lo? Mee yidmeh lach? Oomee yishveh lach? Oomee ya-aroch lach? Ha-Ayl, ha-gadol, ha-geebor, v'ha-nora, Ayl elyon, konay sha-ma-yim va-aretz. N'ha-lel-cha, oon-sha-bay-chacha, oon-fa-ercha, oon-varaych et shaym kod-shecha. Ka-amoor: L'Dovid. Bar'chee, nafshee, et Ado-nai, v'chol k'ra-vai, et shaym kadsho.

As it is written: "All my bones will say, 'God, who is like You? Who saves the poor man from one that is stronger than him or the poor and the needy from one who wishes to rob him?'" Who is like You? Who is equal to You? Who can be compared to You? The great, mighty, awesome God, lofty God, Creator of heaven and earth. We will praise You, acclaim You, glorify You and bless Your holy name. As it is said: Of David. "Bless, the Lord, O my soul, and all that is within me, bless His holy name."

הָאֵל בְּתַעֲצֻמוֹת עֻזֶּךָ, הַגָּדוֹל בִּכְבוֹד שְׁמֶךָ. הַגִּבּוֹר לָנֶצַח וְהַנּוֹרָא בְּנוֹרְאוֹתֶיךָ. הַמֶּלֶךְ הַיּוֹשֵׁב עַל כִּסֵּא רָם וְנִשָּׂא:

Ha-Ayl b'ta-atzoomot oo-zecha. Ha-gadol bich-vod sh'mecha. Ha-geebor la-netzach, v'ha-nora b'nor'o-techa! Ha-melech ha-yoshayv al keesay ram v'neesa!

O God in the strength of Your power. Great in the honor of Your name. Strong forever, and awesome in Your awesome deeds! The King Who sits on a high and lofty throne!

שׁוֹכֵן עַד, מָרוֹם וְקָדוֹשׁ שְׁמוֹ: וְכָתוּב, רַנְּנוּ צַדִּיקִים בַּיְיָ, לַיְשָׁרִים נָאוָה תְהִלָּה. בְּפִי יְשָׁרִים תִּתְהַלָּל. וּבְדִבְרֵי צַדִּיקִים תִּתְבָּרַךְ. וּבִלְשׁוֹן חֲסִידִים תִּתְרוֹמָם. וּבְקֶרֶב קְדוֹשִׁים תִּתְקַדָּשׁ:

Shochayn ad, marom v'kadosh sh'mo! V'chatoov: Ran'noo, tzadeekim, bado-nai, lai-sha-rim navah t'hee-lah. B'fee y'sha-rim tithalal, oov-divray tzadeekim tit-barach, oovil-shon cha-seedim tit-romam, oov-kerev k'doshim tit-kadash.

The One Who dwells for eternity, exalted and holy is His name! And it is written: "Rejoice in the Lord, O you righteous, praise is comely to the upright." In the mouths of the upright You will be praised, and in the words of the righteous You will be blessed, and in the tongues of the pious You will be exalted, and in the midst of the holy You will be sanctified.

וּבְמַקְהֲלוֹת רִבְבוֹת עַמְּךָ בֵּית יִשְׂרָאֵל, בְּרִנָּה יִתְפָּאַר שִׁמְךָ מַלְכֵּנוּ, בְּכָל דּוֹר וָדוֹר, שֶׁכֵּן חוֹבַת כָּל הַיְצוּרִים, לְפָנֶיךָ יְיָ אֱלֹהֵינוּ, וֵאלֹהֵי אֲבוֹתֵינוּ, לְהוֹדוֹת לְהַלֵּל לְשַׁבֵּחַ לְפָאֵר לְרוֹמֵם לְהַדֵּר לְבָרֵךְ לְעַלֵּה וּלְקַלֵּס, עַל כָּל דִּבְרֵי שִׁירוֹת וְתִשְׁבְּחוֹת דָּוִד בֶּן יִשַׁי עַבְדְּךָ מְשִׁיחֶךָ:

Oovmak-halot riv'vot am'cha, bayt yisra-ayl, b'reenah yit-pa-ar shim-cha, mal-kaynoo, b'chol dor va-dor; she-kayn chovat kol ha-y' tzoorim l'fa-necha, Ado-nai, Elo-haynoo vaylo-hay avotaynoo, l'hodot, l'hallel, l'shabay-ach, l'fa-ayr, l'romaym, l'hadayr, l'varaych, l'alay, ool-kalayss, al kol divray shee-rot v'tishb'chot Da-vid, ben Yeeshai, avd'cha, m'shee-checha.

And in the assemblies of the myriads of Your people, the House of Israel, Your name, our King, will be glorified with song in every generation; for such is the obligation of all creations, Lord, our God and the God of our fathers, to offer thanks, praise, and tribute, to glorify, exalt, revere, bless, elevate, and adore You, beyond all the words of songs and praises of David, son of Jesse, Your servant, Your anointed one.

יִשְׁתַּבַּח שִׁמְךָ לָעַד מַלְכֵּנוּ, הָאֵל הַמֶּלֶךְ הַגָּדוֹל וְהַקָּדוֹשׁ בַּשָּׁמַיִם וּבָאָרֶץ. כִּי לְךָ נָאֶה, יְיָ אֱלֹהֵינוּ וֵאלֹהֵי אֲבוֹתֵינוּ: שִׁיר וּשְׁבָחָה, הַלֵּל וְזִמְרָה, עֹז וּמֶמְשָׁלָה, נֶצַח, גְּדֻלָּה וּגְבוּרָה, תְּהִלָּה וְתִפְאֶרֶת, קְדֻשָּׁה וּמַלְכוּת. בְּרָכוֹת וְהוֹדָאוֹת מֵעַתָּה וְעַד עוֹלָם. בָּרוּךְ אַתָּה יְיָ, אֵל מֶלֶךְ גָּדוֹל בַּתִּשְׁבָּחוֹת אֵל הַהוֹדָאוֹת אֲדוֹן הַנִּפְלָאוֹת הַבּוֹחֵר בְּשִׁירֵי זִמְרָה מֶלֶךְ אֵל חֵי הָעוֹלָמִים.

Yishtabach shimcha la-ad, Malkay-noo, ha-Ayl ha-melech, ha-gadol v'ha-kadosh ba-shamayim oova-aretz, ki l'cha na-eh, Ado-nai, Elo-haynoo vaylohay avo-taynoo, sheer oosh-vacha, halayl v'zimrah, oz oo-mem-shalah, netzach, g'doolah oog-voorah, t'heelah v'tif-eret, k'dooshah oo-malchut, b'rachot v'hoda-ot, mey-atah v'ad olam. Baruch atah, Ado-

May Your name be praised forever, our King, God and King, great and holy in heaven and earth, for to You is befitting, Lord, our God and God of our fathers, song and praise, acclaim and melody, strength and rulership, victory, greatness and might, praise and glory, holiness and kingship, blessings and thanksgivings, from now and forever. Blessed are You, Lord, God, King great in praises, the

nai, El, melech, gadol batishbachot, El hahoda-ot, Adon hanifla-ot, habochayr b'sheeray zimrah, Melech, El, chay ha-olamim.

God to whom we owe thanks, the Master of wonders, Who is pleased with melodious song, the King, the God, Life of the worlds.

While reclining on our left side we raise the cup of wine,
recite the following blessing and drink the fourth cup of wine.

בָּרוּךְ אַתָּה יְיָ, אֱלֹהֵינוּ מֶלֶךְ הָעוֹלָם, בּוֹרֵא פְּרִי הַגָּפֶן:

We now recite the following, adding the sentence in parentheses on Shabbat:

בָּרוּךְ אַתָּה יְיָ אֱלֹהֵינוּ מֶלֶךְ הָעוֹלָם עַל הַגֶּפֶן וְעַל פְּרִי הַגֶּפֶן. וְעַל תְּנוּבַת הַשָּׂדֶה, וְעַל אֶרֶץ חֶמְדָּה טוֹבָה וּרְחָבָה, שֶׁרָצִיתָ וְהִנְחַלְתָּ לַאֲבוֹתֵינוּ, לֶאֱכוֹל מִפִּרְיָהּ וְלִשְׂבּוֹעַ מִטּוּבָהּ. רַחֵם נָא יְיָ אֱלֹהֵינוּ עַל יִשְׂרָאֵל עַמֶּךָ, וְעַל יְרוּשָׁלַיִם עִירֶךָ, וְעַל צִיּוֹן מִשְׁכַּן כְּבוֹדֶךָ, וְעַל מִזְבְּחֶךָ וְעַל הֵיכָלֶךָ. וּבְנֵה יְרוּשָׁלַיִם עִיר הַקֹּדֶשׁ בִּמְהֵרָה בְיָמֵינוּ, וְהַעֲלֵנוּ לְתוֹכָהּ, וְשַׂמְּחֵנוּ בְּבִנְיָנָהּ וְנֹאכַל מִפִּרְיָהּ וְנִשְׂבַּע מִטּוּבָהּ, וּנְבָרֶכְךָ עָלֶיהָ בִּקְדֻשָּׁה וּבְטָהֳרָה (וּרְצֵה וְהַחֲלִיצֵנוּ בְּיוֹם הַשַּׁבָּת הַזֶּה) וְשַׂמְּחֵנוּ בְּיוֹם חַג הַמַּצּוֹת הַזֶּה. כִּי אַתָּה יְיָ טוֹב וּמֵטִיב לַכֹּל, וְנוֹדֶה לְּךָ עַל הָאָרֶץ וְעַל פְּרִי הַגָּפֶן. בָּרוּךְ אַתָּה יְיָ, עַל הָאָרֶץ וְעַל פְּרִי הַגָּפֶן:

Baruch atah, Ado-nai, Elo-haynoo, melech ha-olam, boray p'ree haga-fen.

Blessed are You, Lord, our God, King of the universe, Who created the fruit of the vine.

Baruch atah, Ado-nai, Elo-haynoo, melech ha-olam, al ha-gefen v'al p'ree ha-gefen v'al t'noovat ha-sadeh, v'al eretz chemdah, tovah, oor-chavah, shera-tzeeta v'hinchalta la-avotaynoo, le-echol mee-peeryah v'lisbo-a mee-toovah. Rachaym na, Ado-nai, Elo-haynoo, al yisra-ayl a-mecha, v'al y'roosha-la-yim ee-recha, v'al tzee-on mishkan k'vo-decha, v'al mizb'checha, v'al hay-

Blessed are You, Lord, our God, King of the universe, for the vine and for the fruit of the vine and for the produce of the field, and for the desirable, good, and spacious land, which You were pleased to give as a heritage to our forefathers, to eat of its fruit and to become satisfied from its goodness. Have mercy, Lord, our God, upon Israel Your people, upon Jerusalem Your city, upon Mount Zion the dwelling place of Your glory, upon

cha-lecha. Oov-nay y'roosha-la-yim eer ha-ko-desh, bim-hayra v'ya-maynoo. V'ha-alaynoo l'tochah v'sam'chaynoo b'vinyanah. V'nochal mee-peeryah v'nisba mee-toovah. Oon-va-rech'cha a-leha bik-doosha oov-taharah. (Oor-tzay v'hacha-lee-tzaynoo b'yom ha-shabbat ha-zeh,) v'samchaynu b'yom chag hamatzos hazeh. Kee atah, Ado-nai, tov oomaytiv la-kol, v'nodeh l'cha al ha-aretz v'al p'ree ha-gafen. Baruch atah, Ado-nai, al ha-aretz v'al p'ree ha-gafen.

Your altar, and upon Your Temple. Rebuild Jerusalem the holy city, quickly in our days. Bring us up there and make us happy in its rebuilding. Let us eat of its fruit and become satisfied from its goodness. And we will bless You for it, in holiness and purity. (And may it be acceptable to You, that You strengthen us on this Sabbath day,) and cause us to rejoice on this holiday of Matzot. For You, O Lord, are good and kind to all, and we thank You for the land and the fruit of the vine. Blessed are You, Lord, for the land and for the fruit of the vine.

נרצה

Nirtzah

Our seder service is accepted

With *Nirtzah,* our seder service is accepted and concluded. We sing the final songs. There are many musical traditions for these songs, depending on country or region of origin, or family custom. This closing section contains some of the most well-known songs of the Passover seder.

חֲסַל סִדּוּר פֶּסַח כְּהִלְכָתוֹ, כְּכָל מִשְׁפָּטוֹ וְחֻקָתוֹ. כַּאֲשֶׁר זָכִינוּ לְסַדֵּר אוֹתוֹ, כֵּן נִזְכֶּה לַעֲשׂוֹתוֹ. זָךְ שׁוֹכֵן מְעוֹנָה, קוֹמֵם קְהַל עֲדַת מִי מָנָה. בְּקָרוֹב נַהֵל נִטְעֵי כַנָּה, פְּדוּיִם לְצִיּוֹן בְּרִנָּה.

⏳ Jerusalem means "the city of peace." With Nirtzah, we have come full circle, and our eyes turn to the city of peace. The various pieces of the Passover puzzle have given way to a brilliant singularity of vision–of Jerusalem and of peace. The fruit of freedom is peace–peace within us personally, and peace between us as fellow Jews.

Chasal seedoor pesach k'hil-chato, k'chol mishpato v'chookato. Ka-asher za-cheenoo l'sa-dayr oto, kayn nizkeh la-asoto. Zach shochayn m'onah, komaym k'hal adat mee ma-nah. B'karov na-hayl nit-ay chanah. P'doo-yim l'tzee-on b'reenah.

The Passover service is now completed in accordance with its laws, according to all its regulations and statutes. Just as we have been privileged to arrange it, so may we be privileged to perform it. O Pure One Who dwells in heaven, raise up the assembly of Your innumerable people. Quickly, guide the offshoots of Your stock, redeemed to Zion with joyous song.

לְשָׁנָה הַבָּאָה בִּירוּשָׁלָיִם:

L'shana ha-ba-ah bee-roosha-la-yim! *Next year in Jerusalem!*

The following is said only on the first night of the seder.
On the second night, turn to page 81.

וּבְכֵן "וַיְהִי בַּחֲצִי הַלַּיְלָה".

Oov'chayn vai-hee ba-chatzee ha-lailah. *And so it came to pass at midnight.*

אָז רוֹב נִסִּים הִפְלֵאתָ בַּלַּיְלָה, בְּרֹאשׁ אַשְׁמוּרוֹת זֶה הַלַּיְלָה, גֵּר צֶדֶק נִצַּחְתּוֹ כְּנֶחֱלַק לוֹ לַיְלָה, וַיְהִי בַּחֲצִי הַלַּיְלָה.

Az, rov nee-sim hiflayta ba-laila. B'rosh ashmoo-rot zeh ha-lailah, ger tzedek nee-tzachto k'ne-chelak lo lailah. Vai-hee ba-chatzee ha-lailah.

Previously, You performed many miracles at night. At the start of the watch of this night, You caused the righteous convert (Abraham) to be victorious when he divided (his camp) at night. It came to pass at midnight.

דַּנְתָּ מֶלֶךְ גְּרָר בַּחֲלוֹם הַלַּיְלָה, הִפְחַדְתָּ אֲרַמִּי בְּאֶמֶשׁ לַיְלָה, וַיָּשַׂר יִשְׂרָאֵל לְמַלְאָךְ וַיּוּכַל לוֹ לַיְלָה, וַיְהִי בַּחֲצִי הַלַּיְלָה.

Danta melech G'rar ba-chalom ha-lailah. Hifchad'ta aramee b'emesh lailah. Va-yasar yisra-ayl l'mal-ach va-yoochal lo lailah. Vai-hee ba-chatzee ha-lailah.

You judged the king of Gerar (Abimelech) in a dream at night. You frightened (Laban) the Aramean in the night. And Israel wrestled with the angel and overcame him at night. It came to pass at midnight.

זֶרַע בְּכוֹרֵי פַתְרוֹס מָחַצְתָּ בַּחֲצִי הַלַּיְלָה, חֵילָם לֹא מָצְאוּ בְּקוּמָם בַּלַּיְלָה, טִיסַת נְגִיד חֲרֹשֶׁת סִלִּיתָ בְּכוֹכְבֵי לַיְלָה, וַיְהִי בַּחֲצִי הַלַּיְלָה.

Zera b'choray fatros machatz-ta ba-chatzee ha-lailah. Chaylam lo matz'oo b'koomam ba-lailah. Teesat n'gid cha-roshet seeleeta b'choch'-vay lailah. Vai-hee ba-chatzee ha-lailah.

You destroyed the firstborn of the Egyptians in the dark of the night. They did not find their wealth when they arose at night. The army of the prince of Charosheth (Sisera) You swept away with the stars of night. It came to pass at midnight.

יָעַץ מְחָרֵף לְנוֹפֵף אִוּוּי, הוֹבַשְׁתָּ פְגָרָיו בַּלַּיְלָה, כָּרַע בֵּל וּמַצָּבוֹ בְּאִישׁוֹן לַיְלָה, לְאִישׁ חֲמוּדוֹת נִגְלָה רָז חֲזוֹת לַיְלָה, וַיְהִי בַּחֲצִי הַלַּיְלָה.

Ya-atz m'cha-rayf l'nofayf eevooy hovashta p'garav ba-lailah. Kara bayl oo-matzavo b'eeshon lailah. L'ish chamoo-dot niglah raz chazot

When the blasphemer (Sancherib) thought to assail Your Temple, You frustrated him with the corpses (of his army) at night. Bel and his pedestal were humbled in

lailah. Vai-hee ba-chatzee ha-lailah.

the darkness of night. To the man of Your favor (Daniel) the secret vision was revealed at night. It came to pass at midnight.

מִשְׁתַּכֵּר בִּכְלֵי קֹדֶשׁ נֶהֱרַג בּוֹ בַּלַּיְלָה, נוֹשַׁע מִבּוֹר אֲרָיוֹת פּוֹתֵר בְּעוּתֵי לַיְלָה. שִׂנְאָה נָטַר אֲגָגִי וְכָתַב סְפָרִים לַיְלָה, וַיְהִי בַּחֲצִי הַלַּיְלָה.

Mish-ta-kayr bich-lay ko-desh ne-herag bo ba-lailah. Nosha mee-bor ara-yot potayr bee-atootay lailah. Sinnah natar aga-gee v'katav s'farim ba-lailah. Vai-hee ba-chatzee ha-lailah.

He who became drunk (Belshazzer) from the holy vessels was killed at night. He who was saved from the den of lions (Daniel) interpreted the frightening dreams of the night. The Agagite (Haman) bore hatred and wrote letters at night. It came to pass at midnight.

עוֹרַרְתָּ נִצְחֲךָ עָלָיו בְּנֶדֶד שְׁנַת לַיְלָה, פּוּרָה תִדְרוֹךְ לְשׁוֹמֵר מַה מִלַּיְלָה, צָרַח כַּשֹּׁמֵר וְשָׂח אָתָא בֹקֶר וְגַם לַיְלָה, וַיְהִי בַּחֲצִי הַלַּיְלָה.

O-rarta nitz-chacha alav b'ne-der sh'nat lailah. Poo-rah tidroch l'shomayr mah mee-lailah. Tzarach kasho-mayr v'sach ata bo-ker v'gam lailah. Vai-hee ba-chatzee ha-lailah.

You awakened Your victory over him (Haman) when You disturbed (the king's) sleep at night. You will tread the wine-press for those who ask the watchman "What of the long night." He will shout like a watchman and say, "Morning has come, just as night." It came to pass at midnight.

קָרֵב יוֹם אֲשֶׁר הוּא לֹא יוֹם וְלֹא לַיְלָה, רָם הוֹדַע כִּי לְךָ הַיּוֹם אַף לְךָ הַלַּיְלָה, שׁוֹמְרִים הַפְקֵד לְעִירְךָ כָּל הַיּוֹם וְכָל הַלַּיְלָה, תָּאִיר כְּאוֹר יוֹם חֶשְׁכַת לַיְלָה, וַיְהִי בַּחֲצִי הַלַּיְלָה:

Ka-rayv yom asher hoo lo yom v'lo lailah. Ram! Hoda kee l'cha ha-yom af l'cha ha-lailah. Shom-reem haf-kayd l'eercha, kol ha-yom v'chol ha-lailah. Ta-eer, k'or yom, chesh-kat lailah. Vai-hee ba-chatzee ha-lailah.

Bring near the day which is neither day nor night. O Exalted One! Make known that Yours is the day as well as the night. Appoint watchmen for Your city, all day and all night. Illuminate, as the light of day, the darkness of night. It came to pass at midnight.

The following is said only on the second night of the seder.

וּבְכֵן "וַאֲמַרְתֶּם זֶבַח פֶּסַח".

Oov'chayn va-amartem: Zevach pesach.

And you shall say: "This is the sacrifice of Passover."

אֹמֶץ גְּבוּרוֹתֶיךָ הִפְלֵאתָ בַּפֶּסַח, בְּרֹאשׁ כָּל מוֹעֲדוֹת נִשֵּׂאתָ פֶּסַח, גִּלִּיתָ לְאֶזְרָחִי חֲצוֹת לֵיל פֶּסַח, וַאֲמַרְתֶּם זֶבַח פֶּסַח.

O-metz g'vooro-techa hiflayta ba-pesach. B'rosh kol mo-adot nee-sayta pesach. Geeleeta l'ezrachee chatzot layl pesach. Va-amartem: Zevach pesach.

You demonstrated the strength of Your power on Passover. Above all festivals You raised Passover. You revealed to Abraham what would happen at midnight on Passover. And you shall say: "This is the sacrifice of Passover."

דְּלָתָיו דָּפַקְתָּ כְּחֹם הַיּוֹם בַּפֶּסַח, הִסְעִיד נוֹצְצִים עֻגוֹת מַצּוֹת בַּפֶּסַח, וְאֶל הַבָּקָר רָץ זֵכֶר לְשׁוֹר עֶרֶךְ פֶּסַח, וַאֲמַרְתֶּם זֶבַח פֶּסַח.

D'latav dafakta k'chom ha-yom ba-pesach. Hiss-eed notz'tzim oogot matzot ba-pesach v'el ha-bakar ratz, zaycher l'shor ay-rech pesach. Va-amartem: Zevach pesach.

You knocked at Abraham's door in the heat of the day on Passover. He fed angels with matzot on Passover and he ran to the cattle, in remembrance of the sacrificial ox of Passover. And you shall say: "This is the sacrifice of Passover."

זֹעֲמוּ סְדוֹמִים וְלֹהֲטוּ בָּאֵשׁ בַּפֶּסַח, חֻלַּץ לוֹט מֵהֶם, וּמַצּוֹת אָפָה בְּקֵץ פֶּסַח, טִאטֵאתָ אַדְמַת מֹף וְנֹף בְּעָבְרְךָ בַּפֶּסַח, וַאֲמַרְתֶּם זֶבַח פֶּסַח.

Zo-amoo s'domim v'lo-hatoo ba-aysh ba-pesach. Choolatz lot mayhem oo-matzot afah b'kaytz pesach. Tee-tayta ad'mat mof v'nof b'av-r'cha ba-pesach. Va-amartem: Zevach pesach.

The Sodomites enraged God and were destroyed by fire on Passover. Lot was separated from them and baked matzot at the start of Passover. You swept clean the land of Mof and Nof (in Egypt) when you passed through it on Passover. And you shall say: "This is the sacrifice of Passover."

יָהּ, רֹאשׁ כָּל אוֹן מָחַצְתָּ בְּלֵיל שִׁמּוּר פֶּסַח, כַּבִּיר, עַל בֵּן בְּכוֹר פָּסַחְתָּ בְּדַם פֶּסַח, לְבִלְתִּי תֵּת מַשְׁחִית לָבֹא בִּפְתָחַי בַּפֶּסַח, וַאֲמַרְתֶּם זֶבַח פֶּסַח.

Yah, rosh kol on machatz-ta b'layl sheemoor pesach. Ka-beer! Al bayn b'chor pa-sachta b'dam pesach, l'viltee tayt mash-chit lavo bif-ta-chai ba-pesach. Va-amartem: Zevach pesach.

You, God, destroyed each firstborn on the watchful night of Passover. Mighty One! You passed over Your own firstborn, because of the blood of the sacrifice of Passover, not allowing the destroyer to enter my doors on Passover. And you shall say: "This is the sacrifice of Passover."

מִסְגֶּרֶת סֻגְּרָה בְּעִתּוֹתֵי פֶּסַח, נִשְׁמְדָה מִדְיָן בִּצְלִיל שְׂעוֹרֵי עֹמֶר פֶּסַח, שֹׂרְפוּ מִשְׁמַנֵּי פוּל וְלוּד בִּיקַד יְקוֹד פֶּסַח, וַאֲמַרְתֶּם זֶבַח פֶּסַח.

M'soo-geret soo-garah b'ee-totay pesach. Nish-m'da midyan bitz'lil s'oray, omer, pesach. Sor'foo mishma-nay pool v'lood beekad y'kod pesach. Va-amartem: Zevach pesach.

The walled city of Jericho was besieged on Passover. Midian was destroyed by a cake of barley, the offering of the Omer, on Passover. The chiefs of Pul and Lud were burned in a great fire on Passover. And you shall say: "This is the sacrifice of Passover."

עוֹד הַיּוֹם בְּנֹב לַעֲמֹד, עַד גָּעָה עוֹנַת פֶּסַח, פַּס יָד כָּתְבָה לְקַעֲקֵעַ צוּל בַּפֶּסַח, צָפֹה הַצָּפִית עָרוֹךְ הַשֻּׁלְחָן, בַּפֶּסַח, וַאֲמַרְתֶּם זֶבַח פֶּסַח.

Od ha-yom b'nov la-amod, ad ga-a onat pesach. Pas yad kat'vah l'ka-akay-a tzool ba-pesach, tzafo hatza-feet aroch ha-shoolchan ba-pesach. Va-amartem: Zevach pesach.

He (Sancherib) intended to be that day in Nob, and wait for the coming of Passover. A hand wrote the fate of Zul (Babylon) on Passover, just when the watch was set and the table was spread on Passover. And you shall say: "This is the sacrifice of Passover."

קָהֵל כִּנְּסָה הֲדַסָּה צוֹם לְשַׁלֵּשׁ בַּפֶּסַח, רֹאשׁ מִבֵּית רָשָׁע מָחַצְתָּ בְּעֵץ חֲמִשִּׁים בַּפֶּסַח, שְׁתֵּי אֵלֶּה רֶגַע, תָּבִיא לְעוּצִית בַּפֶּסַח, תָּעֹז יָדְךָ וְתָרוּם יְמִינֶךָ, כְּלֵיל הִתְקַדֶּשׁ חַג פֶּסַח, וַאֲמַרְתֶּם זֶבַח פֶּסַח.

Ka-hal kin'sah hadassah tzom l'sha-laysh ba-pesach. Rosh meebayt rasha, machatz-ta b'aytz chameeshim ba-pesach. Sh'tay ay-leh re-ga ta-vee l'ootzit ba-pesach. Ta-oz yad'cha, v'ta-room y'min'cha, k'layl hit-ka-daysh chag pesach. Va-amartem: Zevach pesach.

Hadassah (Esther) assembled the congregation for a three-day fast on Passover. The head of the evil house (Haman), You hung on a fifty-cubit gallows on Passover. These two misfortunes You shall suddenly bring upon Utzith (Edom) on Passover. May Your hand be strong, and Your right arm uplifted, as on the night when You sanctified the festival of Passover. And you shall say: "This is the sacrifice of Passover."

On both nights, continue here:

כִּי לוֹ נָאֶה, כִּי לוֹ יָאֶה.

Kee lo na-eh! Kee lo ya-eh!

To Him praise is becoming! To Him praise is fitting!

אַדִּיר בִּמְלוּכָה, בָּחוּר כַּהֲלָכָה, גְּדוּדָיו יֹאמְרוּ לוֹ: לְךָ וּלְךָ, לְךָ כִּי לְךָ, לְךָ אַף לְךָ, לְךָ יְיָ הַמַּמְלָכָה. כִּי לוֹ נָאֶה, כִּי לוֹ יָאֶה.

A-deer bim-loocha, bachoor ka-hala-cha. G'doo-dav yom'roo lo: L'cha oo-l'cha, l'cha, kee l'cha, l'cha, af l'cha. L'cha, Ado-nai, ha-mamlacha. Kee lo na-eh! Kee lo ya-eh!

Mighty in kingship, truly chosen. His hosts of angels say to Him: "To You and to You, To You, indeed to You, To You, certainly to You. To You, God, is the sovereignty." To Him praise is becoming! To Him praise is fitting!

דָּגוּל בִּמְלוּכָה, הָדוּר כַּהֲלָכָה, וָתִיקָיו יֹאמְרוּ לוֹ: לְךָ וּלְךָ, לְךָ כִּי לְךָ, לְךָ אַף לְךָ, לְךָ יְיָ הַמַּמְלָכָה. כִּי לוֹ נָאֶה, כִּי לוֹ יָאֶה.

Da-gool bim-loocha, ha-door ka-hala-cha. Va-teekav yom'roo lo: L'cha oo-l'cha, l'cha, kee l'cha, l'cha, af l'cha. L'cha, Ado-nai, ha-mamlacha. Kee lo na-eh! Kee lo ya-eh!

Foremost in kingship, truly glorious, His worthy ones say to Him: "To You and to You, To You, indeed to You, To You, certainly to You. To You, God, is the sovereignty." To Him praise is becoming! To Him praise is fitting!

זַכַּאי בִּמְלוּכָה, חָסִין כַּהֲלָכָה, טַפְסְרָיו יֹאמְרוּ לוֹ: לְךָ וּלְךָ, לְךָ כִּי לְךָ, לְךָ אַף לְךָ, לְךָ יְיָ הַמַּמְלָכָה. כִּי לוֹ נָאֶה, כִּי לוֹ יָאֶה.

Za-kai bim-loocha, cha-sin ka-hala-cha. Taf-s'rav yom'roo lo: L'cha oo-l'cha, l'cha, kee l'cha, l'cha, af l'cha. L'cha, Ado-nai, ha-mamlacha. Kee lo na-eh! Kee lo ya-eh!

Faultless in kingship, truly strong, His angels say to Him: "To You and to You, To You, indeed to You, To You, certainly to You. To You, God, is the sovereignty." To Him praise is becoming! To Him praise is fitting!

יָחִיד בִּמְלוּכָה, כַּבִּיר כַּהֲלָכָה, לִמּוּדָיו יֹאמְרוּ לוֹ: לְךָ וּלְךָ, לְךָ כִּי לְךָ, לְךָ אַף לְךָ, לְךָ יְיָ הַמַּמְלָכָה. כִּי לוֹ נָאֶה, כִּי לוֹ יָאֶה.

Ya-cheed bim-loocha, ka-beer ka-hala-cha. Leemoodav yom'roo lo: L'cha oo-l'cha, l'cha, kee l'cha, l'cha, af l'cha. L'cha, Ado-nai, ha-mamlacha. Kee lo na-eh! Kee lo ya-eh!

Unique in kingship, truly mighty, His disciples say to Him: "To You and to You, To You, indeed to You, To You, certainly to You. To You, God, is the sovereignty." To Him praise is becoming! To Him praise is fitting!

מוֹשֵׁל בִּמְלוּכָה, נוֹרָא כַּהֲלָכָה, סְבִיבָיו יֹאמְרוּ לוֹ: לְךָ וּלְךָ, לְךָ כִּי לְךָ, לְךָ אַף לְךָ, לְךָ יְיָ הַמַּמְלָכָה. כִּי לוֹ נָאֶה, כִּי לוֹ יָאֶה.

Mo-shayl bim-loocha, nora ka-hala-cha. S'vee-vav yom'roo lo: L'cha oo-l'cha, l'cha, kee l'cha, l'cha, af l'cha. L'cha, Ado-nai, ha-mamlacha. Kee lo na-eh! Kee lo ya-eh!

Royal in kingship, truly awesome, those around Him say to Him: "To You and to You, To You, indeed to You, To You, certainly to You. To You, God, is the sovereignty." To Him praise is becoming! To Him praise is fitting!

עָנָו בִּמְלוּכָה, פּוֹדֶה כַּהֲלָכָה, צַדִּיקָיו יֹאמְרוּ לוֹ: לְךָ וּלְךָ, לְךָ כִּי לְךָ, לְךָ אַף לְךָ, לְךָ יְיָ הַמַּמְלָכָה. כִּי לוֹ נָאֶה, כִּי לוֹ יָאֶה.

Anav bim-loocha, podeh ka-hala-cha. Tzadeekav yom'roo lo: L'cha oo-l'cha, l'cha, kee l'cha, l'cha, af l'cha. L'cha, Ado-nai, ha-mamlacha. Kee lo na-eh! Kee lo ya-eh!

Humble in kingship, truly the redeemer, His righteous ones say to Him: "To You and to You, To You, indeed to You, To You, certainly to You. To You, God, is the sovereignty." To Him praise is becoming! To Him praise is fitting!

קָדוֹשׁ בִּמְלוּכָה, רַחוּם כַּהֲלָכָה, שִׁנְאַנָּיו יֹאמְרוּ לוֹ: לְךָ וּלְךָ, לְךָ כִּי לְךָ, לְךָ אַף לְךָ, לְךָ יְיָ הַמַּמְלָכָה. כִּי לוֹ נָאֶה, כִּי לוֹ יָאֶה.

Kadosh bim-loocha, rachoom ka-hala-cha. Shin-anav yom'roo lo: L'cha oo-l'cha, l'cha, kee l'cha, l'cha, af l'cha. L'cha, Ado-nai, ha-mam-lacha. Kee lo na-eh! Kee lo ya-eh!

Holy in kingship, truly merciful, His angels say to Him: "To You and to You, To You indeed to You, To You certainly to You. To You, God, is the sovereignty" To Him praise is becoming! To Him praise is fitting!

תַּקִּיף בִּמְלוּכָה, תּוֹמֵךְ כַּהֲלָכָה, תְּמִימָיו יֹאמְרוּ לוֹ: לְךָ וּלְךָ, לְךָ כִּי לְךָ, לְךָ אַף לְךָ, לְךָ יְיָ הַמַּמְלָכָה. כִּי לוֹ נָאֶה, כִּי לוֹ יָאֶה.

Ta-kif bim-loocha, tomaych ka-hala-cha. T'mee-mav yom'roo lo: L'cha oo-l'cha, l'cha, kee l'cha, l'cha, af l'cha. L'cha, Ado-nai, ha-mam-lacha. Kee lo na-eh! Kee lo ya-eh!

Powerful in kingship, truly sustaining, His perfect ones say to Him: "To You and to You, To You, indeed to You, To You, certainly to You. To You, God, is the sovereignty." To Him praise is becoming! To Him praise is fitting!

אַדִּיר הוּא, יִבְנֶה בֵיתוֹ בְּקָרוֹב, בִּמְהֵרָה בִּמְהֵרָה, בְּיָמֵינוּ בְּקָרוֹב. אֵל בְּנֵה, בְּנֵה בֵיתְךָ בְּקָרוֹב.

A-deer hoo. Yivneh vayto b'karov. Bim-hayra, bim-hayra, b'ya-maynoo b'karov. Ayl b'nay, Ayl b'nay. B'nay vayt-cha b'karov!

Mighty is He. May He rebuild His house soon. Quickly, quickly, in our days soon. God rebuild, God rebuild. Rebuild your House soon!

בָּחוּר הוּא, גָּדוֹל הוּא, דָּגוּל הוּא, יִבְנֶה בֵיתוֹ בְּקָרוֹב, בִּמְהֵרָה בִּמְהֵרָה, בְּיָמֵינוּ בְּקָרוֹב. אֵל בְּנֵה, אֵל בְּנֵה, בְּנֵה בֵיתְךָ בְּקָרוֹב.

Bachoor hoo, gadol hoo, dagool hoo. Yivneh vayto b'karov. Bim-hayra, bim-hayra, b'ya-maynoo b'karov. Ayl b'nay, Ayl b'nay. B'nay vayt-cha b'karov!

Chosen is He. Great is He. Foremost is He. May He rebuild His house soon. Quickly, quickly, in our days soon. God rebuild, God rebuild. Rebuild your House soon!

הָדוּר הוּא, וָתִיק הוּא, זַכַּאי הוּא, חָסִיד הוּא, יִבְנֶה בֵיתוֹ בְּקָרוֹב, בִּמְהֵרָה בִּמְהֵרָה, בְּיָמֵינוּ בְּקָרוֹב. אֵל בְּנֵה, אֵל בְּנֵה, בְּנֵה בֵיתְךָ בְּקָרוֹב.

Hadoor hoo, va-teek hoo, za-kai hoo, cha-seed hoo. Yivneh vayto b'karov. Bim-hayra, bim-hayra, b'ya-maynoo b'karov. Ayl b'nay, Ayl b'nay. B'nay vayt-cha b'karov!

Glorious is He. Worthy is He. Faultless is He. Pious is He. May He rebuild His house soon. Quickly, quickly, in our days soon. God rebuild, God rebuild. Rebuild your House soon!

טָהוֹר הוּא, יָחִיד הוּא, כַּבִּיר הוּא, לָמוּד הוּא, מֶלֶךְ הוּא, נוֹרָא הוּא, סַגִּיב הוּא, עִזּוּז הוּא, פּוֹדֶה הוּא, צַדִּיק הוּא, יִבְנֶה בֵּיתוֹ בְּקָרוֹב, בִּמְהֵרָה בִּמְהֵרָה, בְּיָמֵינוּ בְּקָרוֹב. אֵל בְּנֵה, אֵל בְּנֵה, בְּנֵה בֵיתְךָ בְּקָרוֹב.

Ta-hor hoo, ya-cheed hoo, ka-beer hoo, la-mood hoo, melech hoo, nora hoo, sa-giv hoo, ee-zooz hoo, podeh hoo, tzadeek hoo. Yivneh vayto b'karov. Bim-hayra, bim-hayra, b'ya-maynoo b'karov. Ayl b'nay, Ayl b'nay. B'nay vayt-cha b'karov!

Pure is He. Unique is He. Mighty is He. Wise is He. King is He. Awesome is He. Exalted is He. Strong is He. Redeemer is He. Righteous is He. May He rebuild His house soon. Quickly, quickly, in our days soon. God rebuild, God rebuild. Rebuild your House soon!

קָדוֹשׁ הוּא, רַחוּם הוּא, שַׁדַּי הוּא, תַּקִּיף הוּא, יִבְנֶה בֵּיתוֹ בְּקָרוֹב, בִּמְהֵרָה בִּמְהֵרָה, בְּיָמֵינוּ בְּקָרוֹב. אֵל בְּנֵה, אֵל בְּנֵה, בְּנֵה בֵיתְךָ בְּקָרוֹב.

Kadosh hoo, rachoom hoo, Sha-dai hoo, ta-kif hoo. Yivneh vayto b'karov. Bim-hayra, bim-hayra, b'ya-maynoo b'karov. Ayl b'nay, Ayl b'nay. B'nay vayt-cha b'karov!

Holy is He. Merciful is He. Almighty is He. Powerful is He. May He rebuild His house soon. Quickly, quickly, in our days soon. God rebuild, God rebuild. Rebuild your House soon!

אֶחָד מִי יוֹדֵעַ? אֶחָד אֲנִי יוֹדֵעַ: אֶחָד אֱלֹהֵינוּ שֶׁבַּשָּׁמַיִם וּבָאָרֶץ.

Echad mee yoday-a? Echad a-nee yoday-a! Echad Elo-haynoo she-ba-sha-ma-yim oova-aretz.

Who knows one? I know one! One is our God in heaven and on earth.

שְׁנַיִם מִי יוֹדֵעַ? שְׁנַיִם אֲנִי יוֹדֵעַ: שְׁנֵי לֻחוֹת הַבְּרִית, אֶחָד אֱלֹהֵינוּ שֶׁבַּשָּׁמַיִם וּבָאָרֶץ.

Sh'na-yim mee yoday-a? Sh'na-yim a-nee yoday-a! Sh'nay loo-chot hab'reet. Echad Elo-haynoo she-basha-ma-yim oova-aretz.

Who knows two? I know two! Two are the Tablets of the Covenant. One is our God in heaven and on earth.

שְׁלֹשָׁה מִי יוֹדֵעַ? שְׁלֹשָׁה אֲנִי יוֹדֵעַ: שְׁלֹשָׁה אָבוֹת, שְׁנֵי לֻחוֹת הַבְּרִית, אֶחָד אֱלֹהֵינוּ שֶׁבַּשָּׁמַיִם וּבָאָרֶץ.

Sh'losha mee yoday-a? Sh'losha a-nee yoday-a! Sh'losha avot. Sh'nay loo-chot hab'reet. Echad Elo-haynoo she-basha-ma-yim oova-aretz.

Who knows three? I know three! Three are the Patriarchs. Two are the Tablets of the Covenant. One is our God in heaven and on earth.

אַרְבַּע מִי יוֹדֵעַ? אַרְבַּע אֲנִי יוֹדֵעַ: אַרְבַּע אִמָּהוֹת, שְׁלֹשָׁה אָבוֹת, שְׁנֵי לֻחוֹת הַבְּרִית, אֶחָד אֱלֹהֵינוּ שֶׁבַּשָּׁמַיִם וּבָאָרֶץ.

Arba mee yoday-a? Arba a-nee yoday-a! Arba eema-hot. Sh'losha avot. Sh'nay loo-chot hab'reet. Echad Elo-haynoo she-basha-ma-yim oova-aretz.

Who knows four? I know four! Four are the Matriarchs. Three are the Patriarchs. Two are the Tablets of the Covenant. One is our God in heaven and on earth.

חֲמִשָּׁה מִי יוֹדֵעַ? חֲמִשָּׁה אֲנִי יוֹדֵעַ: חֲמִשָּׁה חוּמְשֵׁי תוֹרָה, אַרְבַּע אִמָּהוֹת, שְׁלֹשָׁה אָבוֹת, שְׁנֵי לֻחוֹת הַבְּרִית, אֶחָד אֱלֹהֵינוּ שֶׁבַּשָּׁמַיִם וּבָאָרֶץ.

Cha-meesha mee yoday-a? Cha-meesha a-nee yoday-a! Cha-meesha choom-shay torah. Arba eema-hot. Sh'losha avot. Sh'nay loo-chot hab'reet. Echad Elo-haynoo she-basha-ma-yim oova-aretz.

Who knows five? I know five! Five are the books of the Torah. Four are the Matriarchs. Three are the Patriarchs. Two are the Tablets of the Covenant. One is our God in heaven and on earth.

שִׁשָּׁה מִי יוֹדֵעַ? שִׁשָּׁה אֲנִי יוֹדֵעַ: שִׁשָּׁה סִדְרֵי מִשְׁנָה, חֲמִשָּׁה חוּמְשֵׁי תוֹרָה, אַרְבַּע אִמָּהוֹת, שְׁלֹשָׁה אָבוֹת, שְׁנֵי לֻחוֹת הַבְּרִית, אֶחָד אֱלֹהֵינוּ שֶׁבַּשָּׁמַיִם וּבָאָרֶץ.

Sheesha mee yoday-a? Sheesha a-nee yoday-a. Sheesha sid-ray mishna. Cha-meesha choom-shay torah. Arba eema-hot. Sh'losha avot. Sh'nay loo-chot hab'reet. Echad Elo-haynoo she-basha-ma-yim oova-aretz.

Who knows six? I know six! Six are the orders of the Mishnah. Five are the books of the Torah. Four are the Matriarchs. Three are the Patriarchs. Two are the Tablets of the Covenant. One is our God in heaven and on earth.

שִׁבְעָה מִי יוֹדֵעַ? שִׁבְעָה אֲנִי יוֹדֵעַ: שִׁבְעָה יְמֵי שַׁבַּתָּא, שִׁשָּׁה סִדְרֵי מִשְׁנָה, חֲמִשָּׁה חוּמְשֵׁי תוֹרָה, אַרְבַּע אִמָּהוֹת, שְׁלֹשָׁה אָבוֹת, שְׁנֵי לֻחוֹת הַבְּרִית, אֶחָד אֱלֹהֵינוּ שֶׁבַּשָּׁמַיִם וּבָאָרֶץ.

Shivah mee yoday-a? Shivah a-nee yoday-a! Shivah y'may shaba-ta. Sheesha sid-ray mishna. Cha-mee-sha choom-shay torah. Arba eema-hot. Sh'losha avot. Sh'nay loo-chot hab'reet. Echad Elo-haynoo she-basha-ma-yim oova-aretz.

Who knows seven? I know seven! Seven are the days of the week. Six are the orders of the Mishnah. Five are the books of the Torah. Four are the Matriarchs. Three are the Patriarchs. Two are the Tablets of the Covenant. One is our God in heaven and on earth.

שְׁמוֹנָה מִי יוֹדֵעַ? שְׁמוֹנָה אֲנִי יוֹדֵעַ: שְׁמוֹנָה יְמֵי מִילָה, שִׁבְעָה יְמֵי שַׁבַּתָּא, שִׁשָּׁה סִדְרֵי מִשְׁנָה, חֲמִשָּׁה חוּמְשֵׁי תוֹרָה, אַרְבַּע אִמָּהוֹת, שְׁלֹשָׁה אָבוֹת, שְׁנֵי לֻחוֹת הַבְּרִית, אֶחָד אֱלֹהֵינוּ שֶׁבַּשָּׁמַיִם וּבָאָרֶץ.

Sh'monah mee yoday-a? Sh'monah a-nee yoday-a! Sh'monah y'may mee-lah. Shivah y'may shaba-ta. Sheesha sid-ray mishna. Cha-meesha choom-shay torah. Arba eema-hot. Sh'losha avot. Sh'nay loo-chot hab'reet. Echad Elo-haynoo she-basha-ma-yim oova-aretz.

Who knows eight? I know eight! Eight are the days for circumcision. Seven are the days of the week. Six are the orders of the Mishnah. Five are the books of the Torah. Four are the Matriarchs. Three are the Patriarchs. Two are the Tablets of the Covenant. One is our God in heaven and on earth.

תִּשְׁעָה מִי יוֹדֵעַ? תִּשְׁעָה אֲנִי יוֹדֵעַ: תִּשְׁעָה יַרְחֵי לֵדָה, שְׁמוֹנָה יְמֵי מִילָה, שִׁבְעָה יְמֵי שַׁבַּתָּא, שִׁשָּׁה סִדְרֵי מִשְׁנָה, חֲמִשָּׁה חוּמְשֵׁי תוֹרָה, אַרְבַּע אִמָּהוֹת, שְׁלֹשָׁה אָבוֹת, שְׁנֵי לֻחוֹת הַבְּרִית, אֶחָד אֱלֹהֵינוּ שֶׁבַּשָּׁמַיִם וּבָאָרֶץ.

Tisha mee yoday-a? Tisha a-nee yoday-a! Tisha yar-chay layda. Sh'monah y'may mee-lah. Shivah y'may shaba-ta. Sheesha sid-ray mishna. Cha-meesha choom-shay torah. Arba eema-hot. Sh'losha avot. Sh'nay loo-chot hab'reet. Echad Elo-haynoo she-basha-ma-yim oova-aretz.

Who knows nine? I know nine! Nine are the months of childbirth. Eight are the days for circumcision. Seven are the days of the week. Six are the orders of the Mishnah. Five are the books of the Torah. Four are the Matriarchs. Three are the Patriarchs. Two are the Tablets of the Covenant. One is our God in heaven and on earth.

עֲשָׂרָה מִי יוֹדֵעַ? עֲשָׂרָה אֲנִי יוֹדֵעַ: עֲשָׂרָה דִבְּרַיָּא, תִּשְׁעָה יַרְחֵי לֵדָה, שְׁמוֹנָה יְמֵי מִילָה, שִׁבְעָה יְמֵי שַׁבַּתָּא, שִׁשָּׁה סִדְרֵי מִשְׁנָה, חֲמִשָּׁה חוּמְשֵׁי תוֹרָה, אַרְבַּע אִמָּהוֹת, שְׁלֹשָׁה אָבוֹת, שְׁנֵי לֻחוֹת הַבְּרִית, אֶחָד אֱלֹהֵינוּ שֶׁבַּשָּׁמַיִם וּבָאָרֶץ.

Asarah mee yoday-a? Asarah a-nee yoday-a! Asarah dib'ra-ya. Tisha yar-chay layda. Sh'monah y'may mee-lah. Shivah y'may shaba-ta. Sheesha sid-ray mishna. Cha-meesha choom-shay torah. Arba eema-hot. Sh'losha avot. Sh'nay loo-chot hab'reet. Echad Elo-haynoo she-basha-ma-yim oova-aretz.

Who knows ten? I know ten! Ten are the commandments. Nine are the months of childbirth. Eight are the days for circumcision. Seven are the days of the week. Six are the orders of the Mishnah. Five are the books of the Torah. Four are the Matriarchs. Three are the Patriarchs. Two are the Tablets of the Covenant. One is our God in heaven and on earth.

אַחַד עָשָׂר מִי יוֹדֵעַ? אַחַד עָשָׂר אֲנִי יוֹדֵעַ: אַחַד עָשָׂר כּוֹכְבַיָּא, עֲשָׂרָה דִבְּרַיָּא, תִּשְׁעָה יַרְחֵי לֵדָה, שְׁמוֹנָה יְמֵי מִילָה, שִׁבְעָה יְמֵי שַׁבַּתָּא, שִׁשָּׁה סִדְרֵי מִשְׁנָה, חֲמִשָּׁה חוּמְשֵׁי תוֹרָה, אַרְבַּע אִמָּהוֹת, שְׁלֹשָׁה אָבוֹת, שְׁנֵי לֻחוֹת הַבְּרִית, אֶחָד אֱלֹהֵינוּ שֶׁבַּשָּׁמַיִם וּבָאָרֶץ.

Achad asar mee yoday-a? Achad asar a-nee yoday-a! Achad asar koch-va-ya. Asarah dib'ra-ya. Tisha yar-chay layda. Sh'monah y'may mee-lah. Shivah y'may shaba-ta. Sheesha sid-ray mishna. Cha-meesha choom-shay torah. Arba eema-hot.

Who knows eleven? I know eleven! Eleven are the stars (in Joseph's dream). Ten are the commandments. Nine are the months of childbirth. Eight are the days for circumcision. Seven are the days of the week. Six are the orders of the Mishnah. Five are the books of the Torah. Four are

Sh'losha avot. Sh'nay loo-chot hab'reet. Echad Elo-haynoo she-basha-ma-yim oova-aretz.

the Matriarchs. Three are the Patriarchs. Two are the Tablets of the Covenant. One is our God in heaven and on earth.

שְׁנֵים עָשָׂר מִי יוֹדֵעַ? שְׁנֵים עָשָׂר אֲנִי יוֹדֵעַ: שְׁנֵים עָשָׂר שִׁבְטַיָּא, אַחַד עָשָׂר כּוֹכְבַיָּא, עֲשָׂרָה דִבְּרַיָּא, תִּשְׁעָה יַרְחֵי לֵדָה, שְׁמוֹנָה יְמֵי מִילָה, שִׁבְעָה יְמֵי שַׁבַּתָּא, שִׁשָּׁה סִדְרֵי מִשְׁנָה, חֲמִשָּׁה חוּמְשֵׁי תוֹרָה, אַרְבַּע אִמָּהוֹת, שְׁלֹשָׁה אָבוֹת, שְׁנֵי לֻחוֹת הַבְּרִית, אֶחָד אֱלֹהֵינוּ שֶׁבַּשָּׁמַיִם וּבָאָרֶץ.

Sh'naym asar mee yoday-a? Sh'naym asar a-nee yoday-a! Sh'naym asar shiv-ta-ya. Achad asar koch-va-ya. Asarah dib'ra-ya. Tisha yar-chay layda. Sh'monah y'may mee-lah. Shivah y'may shaba-ta. Sheesha sid-ray mishna. Cha-meesha choom-shay torah. Arba eema-hot. Sh'losha avot. Sh'nay loo-chot hab'reet. Echad Elo-haynoo she-basha-ma-yim oova-aretz.

Who knows twelve? I know twelve! Twelve are the tribes. Eleven are the stars (in Joseph's dream). Ten are the commandments. Nine are the months of childbirth. Eight are the days for circumcision. Seven are the days of the week. Six are the orders of the Mishnah. Five are the books of the Torah. Four are the Matriarchs. Three are the Patriarchs. Two are the Tablets of the Covenant. One is our God in heaven and on earth.

שְׁלֹשָׁה עָשָׂר מִי יוֹדֵעַ ? שְׁלֹשָׁה עָשָׂר אֲנִי יוֹדֵעַ: שְׁלֹשָׁה עָשָׂר מִדַּיָּא, שְׁנֵים עָשָׂר שִׁבְטַיָּא, אַחַד עָשָׂר כּוֹכְבַיָּא, עֲשָׂרָה דִבְּרַיָּא, תִּשְׁעָה יַרְחֵי לֵדָה, שְׁמוֹנָה יְמֵי מִילָה, שִׁבְעָה יְמֵי שַׁבַּתָּא, שִׁשָּׁה סִדְרֵי מִשְׁנָה, חֲמִשָּׁה חוּמְשֵׁי תוֹרָה, אַרְבַּע אִמָּהוֹת, שְׁלֹשָׁה אָבוֹת, שְׁנֵי לֻחוֹת הַבְּרִית, אֶחָד אֱלֹהֵינוּ שֶׁבַּשָּׁמַיִם וּבָאָרֶץ.

Sh'losha asar mee yoday-a? Sh'losha asar a-nee yoday-a! Sh'losha asar mee-da-ya. Sh'naym asar shiv-ta-ya. Achad asar koch-va-ya. Asarah dib'ra-ya. Tisha yar-chay layda. Sh'monah y'may mee-lah. Shivah y'may shaba-ta. Sheesha sid-

Who knows thirteen? I know thirteen! Thirteen are the attributes of God. Twelve are the tribes. Eleven are the stars (in Joseph's dream). Ten are the commandments. Nine are the months of childbirth. Eight are the days for circumcision. Seven are the days of the week.

ray mishna. Cha-meesha choom-shay torah. Arba eema-hot. Sh'losha avot. Sh'nay loo-chot hab'reet. Echad Elo-haynoo she-basha-mayim oova-aretz.

Six are the orders of the Mishnah. Five are the books of the Torah. Four are the Matriarchs. Three are the Patriarchs. Two are the Tablets of the Covenant. One is our God in heaven and on earth.

חַד גַּדְיָא, חַד גַּדְיָא

דְּזַבִּין אַבָּא בִּתְרֵי זוּזֵי, חַד גַּדְיָא, חַד גַּדְיָא.

Chad gadya, chad gadya, d'za-bin aba bit-ray zoozay. Chad gadya, chad gadya.

One kid, one kid, that father bought for two zuzim. One kid, one kid.

וְאָתָא שׁוּנְרָא, וְאָכְלָה לְגַדְיָא, דְּזַבִּין אַבָּא בִּתְרֵי זוּזֵי, חַד גַּדְיָא, חַד גַּדְיָא.

V'ata shoonra v'ach'la l'gadya d'za-bin aba bit-ray zoozay. Chad gadya, chad gadya.

Then came a cat that ate the kid that father bought for two zuzim. One kid, one kid.

וְאָתָא כַלְבָּא, וְנָשַׁךְ לְשׁוּנְרָא, דְּאָכְלָה לְגַדְיָא, דְּזַבִּין אַבָּא בִּתְרֵי זוּזֵי, חַד גַּדְיָא, חַד גַּדְיָא.

V'ata chalba v'na-shach l'shoonra d'ach'la l'gadya d'za-bin aba bit-ray zoozay. Chad gadya, chad gadya.

Then came a dog that bit the cat that ate the kid that father bought for two zuzim. One kid, one kid.

וְאָתָא חוּטְרָא, וְהִכָּה לְכַלְבָּא, דְּנָשַׁךְ לְשׁוּנְרָא, דְּאָכְלָה לְגַדְיָא, דְּזַבִּין אַבָּא בִּתְרֵי זוּזֵי, חַד גַּדְיָא, חַד גַּדְיָא.

V'ata chootra v'hee-ka l'chalba d'na-shach l'shoonra d'ach'la l'gadya d'za-bin aba bit-ray zoozay. Chad gadya, chad gadya.

Then came a stick that beat the dog that bit the cat that ate the kid that father bought for two zuzim. One kid, one kid.

וְאָתָא נוּרָא, וְשָׂרַף לְחוּטְרָא, דְּהִכָּה לְכַלְבָּא, דְּנָשַׁךְ לְשׁוּנְרָא, דְּאָכְלָה לְגַדְיָא, דְּזַבִּין אַבָּא בִּתְרֵי זוּזֵי, חַד גַּדְיָא, חַד גַּדְיָא.

V'ata noo-ra v'saraf l'chootra d'hee-ka l'chalba d'na-shach l'shoon-ra d'ach'la l'gadya d'za-bin aba bit-ray zoozay. Chad gadya, chad gadya.

Then came a fire that burnt the stick that beat the dog that bit the cat that ate the kid that father bought for two zuzim. One kid, one kid.

וְאָתָא מַיָּא, וְכָבָה לְנוּרָא, דְּשָׂרַף לְחוּטְרָא, דְּהִכָּה לְכַלְבָּא, דְּנָשַׁךְ לְשׁוּנְרָא, דְּאָכְלָה לְגַדְיָא, דְּזַבִּין אַבָּא בִּתְרֵי זוּזֵי, חַד גַּדְיָא, חַד גַּדְיָא.

V'ata ma-ya v'chava l'noo-ra d'saraf l'chootra d'hee-ka l'chalba d'na-shach l'shoonra d'ach'la l'gadya d'za-bin aba bit-ray zoozay. Chad gadya, chad gadya.

Then water came and extinguished the fire that burnt the stick that beat the dog that bit the cat that ate the kid that father bought for two zuzim. One kid, one kid.

וְאָתָא תוֹרָא, וְשָׁתָא לְמַיָּא, דְּכָבָה לְנוּרָא, דְּשָׂרַף לְחוּטְרָא, דְּהִכָּה לְכַלְבָּא, דְּנָשַׁךְ לְשׁוּנְרָא, דְּאָכְלָה לְגַדְיָא, דְּזַבִּין אַבָּא בִּתְרֵי זוּזֵי, חַד גַּדְיָא, חַד גַּדְיָא.

V'ata tora v'shata l'ma-ya d'chava l'noo-ra d'saraf l'chootra d'hee-ka l'chalba d'na-shach l'shoonra d'ach'la l'gadya d'za-bin aba bit-ray zoozay. Chad gadya, chad gadya.

Then came an ox and drank the water that extinguished the fire that burnt the stick that beat the dog that bit the cat that ate the kid that father bought for two zuzim. One kid, one kid.

וְאָתָא הַשּׁוֹחֵט, וְשָׁחַט לְתוֹרָא, דְּשָׁתָא לְמַיָּא, דְּכָבָה לְנוּרָא, דְּשָׂרַף לְחוּטְרָא, דְּהִכָּה לְכַלְבָּא, דְּנָשַׁךְ לְשׁוּנְרָא, דְּאָכְלָה לְגַדְיָא, דְּזַבִּין אַבָּא בִּתְרֵי זוּזֵי, חַד גַּדְיָא, חַד גַּדְיָא.

V'ata ha-sho-chayt v'sha-chat l'to-ra d'shata l'ma-ya d'chava l'noo-ra d'saraf l'chootra d'hee-ka l'chalba d'na-shach l'shoonra d'ach'la l'gadya d'za-bin aba bit-ray zoozay. Chad gadya, chad gadya.

Then came the slaughterer and slaugh-tered the ox that drank the water that extinguished the fire that burnt the stick that beat the dog that bit the cat that ate the kid that father bought for two zuzim. One kid, one kid.

וְאָתָא מַלְאַךְ הַמָּוֶת, וְשָׁחַט לְשׁוֹחֵט, דְּשָׁחַט לְתוֹרָא, דְּשָׁתָא לְמַיָּא, דְּכָבָה לְנוּרָא, דְּשָׂרַף לְחוּטְרָא, דְּהִכָּה לְכַלְבָּא, דְּנָשַׁךְ לְשׁוּנְרָא, דְּאָכְלָה לְגַדְיָא, דְּזַבִּין אַבָּא בִּתְרֵי זוּזֵי, חַד גַּדְיָא, חַד גַּדְיָא.

V'ata malach ha-ma-vet v'sha-chat l'sho-chayt d'sha-chat l'tora d'shata l'ma-ya d'chava l'noo-ra d'saraf l'chootra d'hee-ka l'chalba d'na-shach l'shoonra d'ach'la l'gadya d'za-bin aba bit-ray zoozay. Chad gadya, chad gadya.

Then came the Angel of Death and slew the slaughterer who slaughtered the ox that drank the water that extinguished the fire that burnt the stick that beat the dog that bit the cat that ate the kid that father bought for two zuzim. One kid, one kid.

וְאָתָא הַקָּדוֹשׁ בָּרוּךְ הוּא, וְשָׁחַט לְמַלְאַךְ הַמָּוֶת, דְּשָׁחַט לְשׁוֹחֵט, דְּשָׁחַט לְתוֹרָא, דְּשָׁתָא לְמַיָּא, דְּכָבָה לְנוּרָא, דְּשָׂרַף לְחוּטְרָא, דְּהִכָּה לְכַלְבָּא, דְּנָשַׁךְ לְשׁוּנְרָא, דְּאָכְלָה לְגַדְיָא, דְּזַבִּין אַבָּא בִּתְרֵי זוּזֵי, חַד גַּדְיָא, חַד גַּדְיָא.

V'ata ha-kadosh baruch hoo v'sha-chat l'malach ha-ma-vet d'sha-chat l'sho-chayt d'sha-chat l'tora d'shata l'ma-ya d'chava l'noo-ra d'saraf l'chootra d'hee-ka l'chalba d'na-shach l'shoonra d'ach'la l'gadya d'za-bin aba bit-ray zoozay. Chad gadya, chad gadya.

Then came the Holy One, Blessed be He, and killed the Angel of Death, who slew the slaughterer who slaughtered the ox that drank the water that extinguished the fire that burnt the stick that beat the dog that bit the cat that ate the kid that father bought for two zuzim. One kid, one kid.

THE JERUSALEM

Open House

לינת החסד

About Jerusalem Open House

Dear Friend,

Five years ago Meir B., a lonely, confused 35-year-old man, was wandering the streets of Jerusalem. Hungry, tired and cold, he sat down on a bench to rest. He dreamed of food, steaming hot food that would make the constant hunger pangs disappear. He dreamed of a bed, a soft, downy bed that would soothe his aching bones.

Instead, he was confronted with reality.

"Sorry, you can't stay here. Please leave." Meir heard the words. He saw the face of the officer who was talking to him. Yet he did not move. For where would he go?

The Jerusalem Open House was established with just such individuals in mind. It opened its doors to the Meirs of Jerusalem – the loneliest, most destitute and disoriented members of society. It became their haven, the place to go to when there was nowhere else.

The beautiful city of Jerusalem is, unfortunately, home to hundreds of disturbed, abandoned Jews. Their haunted eyes cry out for help. They beg for simple things: a nourishing meal, a shirt to wear, a hot shower, a soft bed.

The Jerusalem Open House responds to their pleas. Each day they serve about 150 breakfasts and 250 dinners to the hungry. Additionally, they provide clothing and shelter to the most needy of these individuals.

Even more importantly, the Jerusalem Open House staff and volunteers teach these men basic life skills so that a self-supporting future becomes possible for them.

With Pesach nearly here, it is imperative that we support these lost souls. Holidays are a particularly lonely time for people without family or friends. Let us open our hearts to them, just as the Jerusalem Open House opens its doors to them.

Food, clothing and shelter cost money, and funds are low this year. But the number of poor people is not low... the number of the hungry is not low... the number of the homeless is not low... In fact, they have grown and increased!

The Jerusalem Open House must expand. But they don't have the means to do so.

Please help them keep their doors open, wide open. Your support enables another starved soul to be fed, another cold man to be clothed, another homeless person to have a place to lay his head.

This Pesach, as you chant "Kol dichfin yeisei veyeichel," do so with the knowledge that you have, indeed, fed the hungry.

In the merit of this great mitzvah, may you and your family enjoy health, wealth and happiness.
Sincerely,

Rabbi Chaim Cohen
Founder of JOH

כל דכפין ייתי ויאכול
Let all who are hungry come and eat

Rivka

A mother of ten Rivka lives and works in at local store. The wages, unfortunately, are far from enough to pay rent and a few of the bills. In her house the children are hungry. The refrigerator is, literally empty.

Every evening the children come to the obvious place: the warm, welcoming home of Linas HaChesed soup kitchen. When they are done eating they pack up a meal for their mom so that she too, may eat with dignity. Many times she cries when she eats. No those are not tears of sorrow, but those of gratitude and relief. Better days are surly ahead all of them. But for now, another day has passed and everyone is fed. Thank G-D.

Those tears belong to you, for you
were a "feeder of the hungry"

Moishele

A ten-year old child from a home of many children that lost their mother. Moishele is learning Torah most of the day, only to return home hungry. He's yet to have eaten a meal. But Moishele knows exactly where one goes when one is hungry: the Linas HaChesed soup kitchen. There's much to think about – he comes in he eats and his hunger is gone…

Moishele returns home, stretches out on this little bed, says Krias Shma and falls peacefully asleep.

That sleep belongs to you, for you
were a "feeder of the hungry"